Equal Training

An Analysis of Antiwhite Material and Language
Manipulation Tactics Used in American Schools

by Student X.

Table of Contents

Mission Statement

Daily, it becomes visible to more and more of the student body that activist teachers, as well as activist student organizations, are using proven public agitation techniques derived from past Marxist and Communist movements. These agitation techniques are exclusively pointed at the White student body, White cultural norms, White symbols and White society as a whole. The school, as an institution, does not have the ability nor the authority to stop those who have dedicated their time on campus to menacing the White population. Without established resources, the only option White students currently have is to join questionable organizations to seek redress.

This student manual is intended to start the process of forming student organizations and networks that will provide an educated alternative to joining extremist groups and movements. That choice, of joining extremist groups or movements, cannot be the only option for White youth experiencing the negative effects of academic and on-campus targeted agitation, which is being delivered using the massive reach of the education platform.

This student manual will analyze and illustrate common agitation techniques currently used by teachers, on-campus organizations and groups, and encourage more appropriate and uniform reactions benefiting both the students and the education administration overall. As of right now, academic freedom is being abused by social agitators, resulting in negative social effects.

There is a large gap for White students who experience the effects of these agitation techniques, a void of actions they can take for themselves and their fellow like-minded students. There is currently nothing in place to fill that void. Like-minded students must form networks and student organizations to share knowledge and best practices among each other in the hope of undoing these negative social effects and secure a better outcome for those of us who are targeted. We must push to reform the education system from the inside and deliver the learning environment that we all deserve.

A unifying environment must be constructed where White students, who are the targets of these agitation techniques, can freely share their experiences and take the opportunity to learn from one another to deal with the negative effects. Most importantly, they must be able to speak freely among each other without interference from others who frequently participate in the agitation being discussed or who champion the use of these agitation techniques on campus.

This manual is dedicated to you, White students. In America and around the world.

Introduction

Contrary to the way I see the White population portrayed by large media companies, I was born and raised in Los Angeles County. Although that county is large and contains many cities, I never lived in one that was predominately White. Most of the places I have worked and classes I've attended weren't either. So, my experience growing up was quite different from what the general population sees broadcast to them by large media outlets. I was born to a working-class family. Since money was always a concern growing up, I was excited when I reached the age of sixteen and could start working. I waited a few years after graduating high school but once I secured a full-time job that paid enough to cover my rent, I began attending night classes at the local community college while working during the day.

Even though a few years had passed since I was in a classroom, I noticed there was something different about the material being used and something different with some of the teachers promoting it. This was the first time I heard the term "White privilege" or experienced teachers making comments about "White people this" or "White people that" as a formal part of their lesson plan. I also noticed that some classes seemed to have more of a prosecutorial atmosphere, instead of an educational one.

The job I held at the time placed a strong emphasis on treating others with respect and had a code of conduct as well as behavioral standards, which they required all employees to adhere to. Thus, it was after encountering more than one teacher who was behaving this way that I began to wonder about what the rules were for the teachers. I wondered, since teachers are employees of the school, do they also have a similar code of conduct and professional behavioral standards that they must follow?

After analyzing the teaching patterns and the material used in these classes, I compiled a few examples of antiwhite presentations. I filed an official grievance with the office of academic affairs, assuming this would operate similarly to the formal complaints process established at the company I was working for at the time. Instead of being handled with swiftness and professionalism, this began what turned out to be a two-year process of navigating the school administration along with outside institutions in search of a remedy.

The following details are important for any student who wants to create positive institutional change inside of the education system. Ultimately, I was left with the impression that my school did not know how to handle a student who could challenge the material used in a respectful and professional manner. And as a result, they ran me in circles, hoping I would eventually give up. I don't want others to have this same experience. I would like to see those who experience these situations continue to push and succeed at making positive changes inside the education system.

The initial grievance I filed with academic affairs resulted in a meeting that was a little over three hours long. This meeting was with the president of academic affairs as well as an administrator. The meeting had intense moments, but it did not offer a resolution in the end. As it turned out, they did not have the authority to make any changes to the material used on campus or any way of affecting the behavior of the teachers. It was recommended that I request a meeting with the Dean of curriculum to see if there was anything he would do.

The initial meeting with the Dean of curriculum was a little over an hour in length, and he was unable to provide solutions or answers to most of the questions presented, but he did take notes and said he would do his best to follow up and check back with me. We communicated by email over the next few semesters. It was common that I would not receive any information from him unless I sent a reminder email asking for a status update. In the end, even though he was the Dean of curriculum, he explained that it was the curriculum committee who make the decisions and who select the pool of material that teachers choose from. This, then, steers the type of atmosphere created inside of the classrooms. The curriculum committee at my school location does not meet with members of the public or students and they operate behind locked doors so they cannot be confronted or pressured to select a different type of material.

Separately, the Dean explained to me that the behavioral standards for teachers does not apply to the material they select or their lesson plans. They are pretty much free to teach whatever they want, and he cited the policy of academic freedom. The Dean did confirm that the teachers exercising academic freedom are not shielded by the school administration and are left vulnerable to push back from the student body.

This meeting was important because it helped me better understand the structure of the education system. Previously, I was looking at it as one big institution, and I'd thought whoever was in charge had the authority to make changes at any other level below them, but that's not accurate. After this meeting, I understood it was more accurate to think of the school system as three pieces—one piece being the school administration, which handles the business aspect of running the school. The second piece being the body of teachers, which also comprises the curriculum committee, and the third piece being the student body. That said, there is a gap between the school administration and the body of teachers. This means there are certain types of changes the administration does not have the authority to instruct the body of teachers to make. The teachers have academic freedom and can teach whatever they want but are vulnerable to push back from the student body.

Understanding this structure, it became clear to me that it's only the student body, who can apply direct pressure on the body of teachers and the curriculum committee to demand positive changes be made from the inside. The school administration is not supposed to shield the teachers but is expected to protect the students in the event the teacher engages in student retaliation. Due to this structure, this struggle must play out between the students and the teachers.

In addition to this, I spoke with a representative at the AAUP. This representative confirmed what I was told about academic freedom was correct. For the record, I support keeping academic freedom. I also spoke with the state-level curriculum committee and was eventually told that they have no authority over the curriculum committee at my location. I talked to a representative at the chancellor's office for California community colleges, who explained this was outside of their authority.

The representative at the chancellor's office told me that if pursuing a legal remedy, they only have legal requirements to meet on behalf of minorities, not White students. In addition to the avenues just mentioned, my school was kind enough to let me have a meeting with their attorney, who confirmed that the school is only required to take legal actions on behalf of minorities and not White students (more on this later).

With all that said, it seems like great effort has been put in to isolating control of the education system. The curriculum committee operates behind locked doors and does not allow any outside influence, so for locations that have radicals on their curriculum committee, they can't be confronted or pressured to change the literature being selected for use at that location.

The teachers have academic freedom, which enables them to partner with radicals on the curriculum committee to ensure the selected material is widely distributed and taught to the student body at that location. The school administration, where student grievances are directed, claims to have no authority over the curriculum committee or body of teachers. In addition, there is no law on the books that requires the school administration to offer the same protections to White students that they do for minorities. Therefore, they don't.

With this being the case, it seems like the fastest and most efficient way to neutralize radicalized teachers and their agenda is to provide equal training at the student level. The most common tactics they use to agitate the general population and instigate conflict can all be neutralized simply by making them visible to the student body. For the growing number of students who want to challenge these radicals, this manual offers an educated alternative to joining questionable groups or participating in questionable activities. It also encourages students to pressure the school administration to hire teachers who will utilize academic freedom for the purpose of teaching White students about the concepts covered in this student manual.

As well, all of the additional information and discoveries that are compiled moving forward can be shared. Schools who have radicalized teachers on staff or making decisions on the curriculum committee need to take steps and establish dedicated training for White students to ensure they identify who these teachers are and then share the tactics they use on campus with the students.

The following chapters are derived from and based on an analysis of the material I encountered in my classes. These chapters contain concepts for recognizing some of the most common language structures and manipulation tactics that you will see embedded in your school literature, along with examples of the effects they have on the general population. Throughout these concepts, you will see ideas and opportunities where students can take action at their specific school location, as well as ideas and opportunities for local political action.

Group Blame Using Color

One of the more common methods we see used to create group blame or assign guilt to large portions of the population is to refer to people by their color, instead of using something more specific like their cultural, ethnic or tribal identity. Referring to people by their color is a specific language structure that's used to implicate all people(s) and populations within one of the four main color categories. Since all people can be consolidated in to four color categories, when you're writing an article or if you make verbal statements using this language structure, whatever you're discussing will incriminate that entire color category and direct public blame at all of them globally.

When we refer to people by what color they are, it's done based on visual observation. We look at them, and based on their outward appearance, decide which of the four color categories they belong to. These four categories are White, Black, Yellow and Brown people.

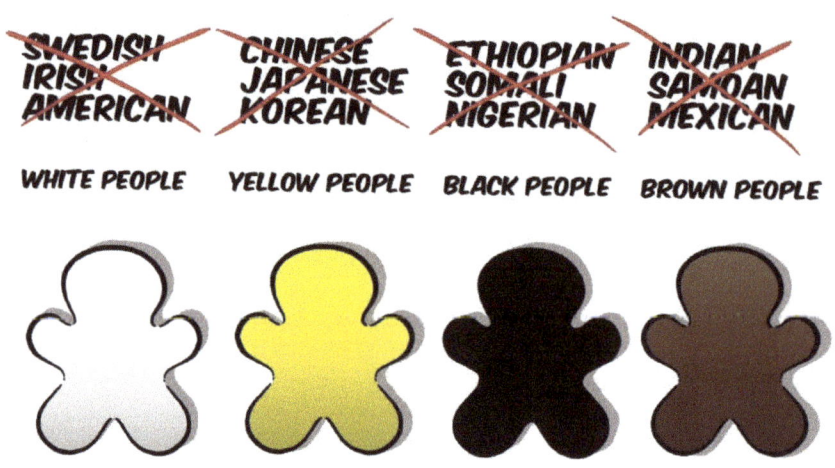

SWEDISH
IRISH
AMERICAN

CHINESE
JAPANESE
KOREAN

ETHIOPIAN
SOMALI
NIGERIAN

INDIAN
SAMOAN
MEXICAN

WHITE PEOPLE   YELLOW PEOPLE   BLACK PEOPLE   BROWN PEOPLE

Uses in Media

Talking this way will cause the same social effects no matter what country you use it in—because referring to people by their color invalidates the different heritages, cultures, and ethnicities around the world. It ignores the differences between these identity categories and refers to a chunk of the planet's population simultaneously, simply based on what color they are. Notice that, when I use the term "Brown people," you won't know which specific society, culture, or ethnic group I'm referencing. If I'm writing an article for a newspaper and reporting on a crime, I can use this language structure for my writing. I can use this tactic as an instrument to assign public blame to every Brown person on the planet, simultaneously. I would do this by referring to the perpetrators in my article by their color, as Brown people, and not by a vague category description like "youths."

If you are one to analyze media reporting, chances are that you've noticed some patterns. You can predict when media will refer to a perpetrator by what color they are, and to create public backlash for that segment of the general population versus when the media will refer to them as a "youth." This referring to the perpetrator as a youth avoids creating the same kind of public backlash for another segment of the population. That said, when we notice that the largest media outlets have all coordinated with each other by using this language structure, for all of the articles they point at the host population of a society, but use a different language structure for all of the articles they point at the other populations, it's obvious that their combined media platform is being used more like a weapon. It's also being used as a tool to create continuous backlash against the host population, instead of as a tool to keep the general population safe and well informed on important matters.

Let's review an example of the social impact it will have to reverse the current media reporting protocol. Instead of referring to members of the host population by their color in every article that's about them, but not the other populations, we're now going to reverse this and refer to all of the other populations by their color in every article that's about them and broadcast that to the general population on a continuous basis. Let's look back at the thousands of media articles that were circulated about major events where the attackers happened to be Brown, like 9/11 or the reports of high-profile shootings that occurred in office buildings, at military bases, at nightclubs, at universities, and so on. Now, keep every sentence of the articles and media talking points the same, just change one word. The one word we'll remove is the description they used for the shooter's identity like "students or coworkers" and insert their color "Brown" there instead. Just think of how different the general populations reaction would be to these exact same events. The language structure of all media reporting, school lesson plans and public talking points would transform from thousands of tiny splintered conversations about students, religious groups or disgruntled coworkers in to one large combined national conversation about "Brown people."

If you had enough control and could use the media platform for this purpose in America, think of how you can condition the general population by continually showering them in articles and talking points to ensure they will hear the term "Brown people" broadcast at them hundreds of times per month. Think of how long-term exposure to this will change the way they're trained to talk to each other in their daily interactions and how they form their thoughts about one another. For example, let's take a society where most people have good manners and commonly refer to different parts of the Brown population by their heritage or ethnic identity. They would typically use terms like Indian, Pakistani, Arab, or Mexican in their daily interactions. Long-term exposure to media that continually broadcast the words "Brown people" at them will eventually retrain the public to stop referring to these inhabitants by their different heritage or ethnic identities and simply call them all "Brown people" instead.

Not only would controlling the language structure used by the media influence what the public thinks about Brown people, but it would also enable them to create a singular reputation for all Brown people worldwide, one where they'd be forced to share in collective blame and guilt. If media outlets were to collectively circulate thousands of articles over a long period of time using the term "Brown people" it would eventually accumulate in the collective mind. It would create a singular reputation for that color category of people, in this case, Brown people. Now, let's analyze media behavior and patterns.

Do we see the largest media companies churning out articles to create the same combined reputation for Brown people that they work to create for White people? No. Do we see the large media companies ensuring the public has the words "Brown people" broadcast at them the same number of times each week that they have the words "White people" broadcast at them? Also no. We don't see the media putting the same money and effort into creating a singular reputation for Brown people that they have created for White people.

For decades, the media has flooded the world with millions of articles using the term "White people" without ever saying which ones. They don't say which national, ethnic, cultural, or tribal groups they are discussing. The result? One singular reputation for "White people" in the collective global mind. Yet, these same media companies and reporters haven't flooded the world with the same number of articles about "Brown people." Therefore, they have not created the same type of combined reputation for Brown people in the collective global mind.

How did they coordinate this? Large media platforms use a different language structure when reporting on events involving

Brown people. They didn't describe them as "Brown". They worded the articles with vague descriptors like students, teens, youths, women and children, protesters, bicycle riders, migrants, coworkers, people searching for a different life, a Florida man, and so on. By using vague descriptors and omitting "Brown," the media reported on events involving people who are Brown without creating the same combined reputation in the global mind about Brown people that they've created for White people.

The power to create public resentment, as well as decide which portion of the population will have public backlash directed at it, rests in the hands of the author. It's the author who determines the way their article will be worded and which descriptions will be used for the people who are involved. If the author is writing an article that will cause protests and public demands for justice from a certain segment of the general population, it's the author who decides if the article will refer to the perpetrator by their color, so the public protests will be directed at all people in that color category, or the author can use a vague description like a "youth" and leave the public protestors with no group of people to direct their demands for "justice" at. In cases like this, it's the author who decides if public protests will be pointed at Brown people or if all Brown people will be provided a free pass, and the person in that article will be described as a "youth" instead.

Take some time to analyze these patterns in media reporting. Now that you know to look for this, pay attention to when the media refers to people by their color instead of using vague descriptors as identifiers. For which of the four color groups has the media built a combined reputation, releasing continuous articles referencing color? To which color groups do they give a free pass by using vague terms like students or teens in their reporting? Count how many times you see the word "White" packed into each article. Do you ever see the words Brown, Black, or Yellow packed into articles the same number of times? Think deeply about why you haven't seen the same large media outlets broadcast reports saying all the same things about Brown, Black, and Yellow people they've said about White people.

Why haven't they flooded the world with an equal number of articles and built the same singular reputation for the other three colors of people they've already created for Whites?

Looking for this pattern and identifying those media outlets and reporters who continually use it and churn out the material makes their agenda visible. They haven't used their platforms to create the same combined reputation for the other three color groups as they have for Whites. Nor have they used their influence to cause the same level of social backlash against the other three colors of people as they have for Whites. This is because their real intention is not to report the news, it's to use their large media platform to attack Whites.

Radicalized authors and news reporters use large media platforms for their own ends. But we must ask, who taught these authors and reporters to write and speak using this language structure? Why has this become the standardized language used by so many of them? The answer is that these people, who work for media outlets, are trained to think, speak and write about their host population this way while they're going through the public school system.

How This Format Is Introduced Using the Education System

This methodology is introduced in the education system using a literary structure that's designed to center all conversations and assignments around a specific color of people. Depending on what country it's in will determine which one of the four color categories is selected so it will reflect on the host population of that country. The justification, I have seen used in the past, is this literature is intended to train the minority groups in that society how to publicly criticize their host population, by using this language structure to form their thinking, writing, verbal remarks and public criticism.

Let's use Mexico as an example. Just imagine the social problems a radicalized teacher could cause once they infiltrate the education system of a predominantly Brown country. Imagine a teacher who wants to use their platform to subvert the Mexican host population or who makes it their life's mission to dissolve the Mexican identity altogether and eventually erase them as a people. They can begin separating the host population of Mexico from its existing Mexican cultural identity by training their students to stop validating it and by calling them something else. Refer to them by their color and start calling them "Brown people" instead of calling them Mexican. This tactic stops acknowledging Mexican identity as being a valid identity and ensures the Mexican people no longer receive validation.

You may wonder, how do they get their students to go along with such a plan? No one asks the students for their opinion, and the teacher never informs them they will be trained to speak, write and think about their host population in this way. Teaching the students to refer to their host population by their color, instead of "Mexican," will run parallel to the main subject being taught in that class.

To condition the students in the habit of using the term "Brown people" for everything and normalizing it in their daily conversations, the teacher simply uses a lesson plan that centers the conversations they have in that classroom around Brown people. Students sign up thinking they're studying a specific subject like Art or History, but the teacher will train them to talk and think differently in a way that runs parallel to that Art or History lesson.

Instead of just studying Art, the teacher will reformat it to study the role of "Brown people" in Art, or the role that "Brownness" plays in Art with the aim of maximizing the number of times the students will need to use the term "Brown people" to complete their writing assignments and classroom conversations. As such, it will become normalized by repetition. The teacher might also require students to use "Brownness" or "Brown people," as instructed in their assignments to receive a passing grade. By the end of that class, the teacher will have a room full of students who have been trained and made to feel comfortable referring to "Brown people" as one single group. The students will start to use "Brown people" in all of their conversations and public criticism, even though the main subject is represented as Art or History.

The wording of educational literature determines how students are trained to talk and structure their thoughts. Long-term exposure to literature using this language structure ensures that children only know how to talk about Mexicans by referring to them as Brown people and no longer using "Mexican." Well-mannered students may have begun that class referring to different parts of the Brown population by their heritage, ethnicity, or cultural identity (like Pakistani, Mexican or Indian).

Still, by the time they come out, they just say Brown people for everything. As a result, those heritages and ethnic or cultural identities are no longer validated or reinforced. Without most students noticing, the teacher can train them to stop referring to their host population as Mexican and start referring to them by their color instead. Since most won't know another way to think, speak or write, the longer this remains the standard structure in school lesson plans, the more likely it is that the teacher succeeds at permanently changing the way the students think, speak and write about their host population.

As far as Mexican cultural identity, it will no longer be validated or attached to the Mexican host population. It will no longer belong to the Mexican people; they'll just be known as Brown people by the generation coming in behind them. Now that it's been separated by the teacher's training in the classroom, the Mexican identity itself can be claimed by other populations, whether they share that heritage, value or protect it, or choose to attack everything it consists of and work to erase it.

Public Shaming and Transferring Blame

Let's look at how this method can be used to publicly blame and transfer guilt to the host population of Mexico for things they didn't do. Imagine a radical teacher begins teaching history in one of the public schools. When putting together a lesson plan, they research historical events they can use to agitate or destabilize their host population. They use this language structure when formatting their school lesson plans. Then, they can take everything they gathered from different populations around the world and develop one combined list of things that have been done by "Brown people" and things that their lesson plan will train the students to publicly criticize Brown people for doing.

Making a lesson plan that uses generic language about Brown people means the students in the class can't tell if the events they learn about were committed by members of their own host population or a group from another part of the world. Their host population is predominantly Brown, so each time they hear or use "Brown people" in their writing and classroom discussions, it will implicate their Mexican host population. This association blames them because they belong to the same color category. It will also shape the opinion of the students taking that class, changing their attitude toward the predominantly Brown inhabitants hosting them. As a result, the students learn to resent their host population.

Ultimately, they will become radicalized and attack their host population.

Take a moment to view this from the side of the host population. Consider the social effects it will create for the general population of Mexico if the children occupying the public school system there are immersed in literature that's structured to use the term "Brown people" thousands of times during their coursework. Think of the rhetoric created inside school classrooms during simple writing assignments or classroom conversations about Brown people. This will eventually spill onto the streets and saturate the entire population of Mexico because this is how teachers have trained children to talk. Aside from permeating their population in generic remarks about Brown people, it will permanently change how their children speak, write and think. It will make agitating and incriminating remarks about Brown people a part of everyday life for the host population of Mexico. It will be everywhere. Inescapable. And if it continues long enough, permanent.

After long-term exposure to the term Brown people from all sides, the Mexicans will eventually become self-destructive. They will suffer the negative social and psychological effects of group guilt, along with public resentment resulting from having this language structure embedded into the public school material and continuously directed at them.

All of the guilting, agitation and social conflict caused by training the children to menace their host population this way will continue until the lesson plans installed by the teacher have been removed and the literature used in public schools is reworded so the children are trained to talk using a different language structure, like referring to their host population as Mexican again, instead of just as Brown people.

Transfer and Circulation

Let's add another layer to this and make it a bit more interesting. Radicalized teachers can take the literature they developed in Mexico to train students to make generic remarks about Brown people and transfer it to any other predominantly Brown country like India (or even a tiny island like Samoa). This material will cause the same social problems for those Brown populations, as it did for the original one. It will have the same effect on any predominantly Brown society, whether a remote island like Samoa or a large country like Mexico because the way it's written will reflect on all Brown people worldwide.

Radical teachers in these countries can form education networks to circulate literature and lesson plans that use this structure from country-to-country and subtly install it into standard curricula one subject at a time. This begins the process of revising the way the children are trained to write, speak and think about their host population. The teachers use these materials as tools to agitate and destabilize the host population from within. To block objections by other academics, they first insert this structure into highly sensitive subjects like ethnic or gender studies. These academics know they can use special treatment policies on racism or hate speech to attack anyone who challenges installing this literature into these subjects.

Let's also point out that the students who take these courses tend to be more emotional than students in other areas of study. The teacher often incentivizes these students to vent their frustrations on the host population. They encourage them to weaponize this tactic in the most aggressive way possible, both when completing writing assignments or when participating in public demonstrations.

Let's take a closer look at how quickly this spreads. Generic criticism of one color category, will include all host populations around the world that fall into that color category, whether their specific population was involved in the topic at hand or not. Once students who speak, write, and think this way enter the workforce, this language structure diffuses into all aspects of society. This becomes the language structure used in mainstream media reporting, the legal system, politics, and all other aspects of social life. The host population of any country this is released in will be saturated in a language structure designed to create resentment against it. This resentment is inflamed by every article, school lesson plan, public conversation, social media post, and lawsuit. As this material compounds over time, the host population is eventually overwhelmed by a tidal wave of verbal attacks and public resentment on all sides.

You can see how quietly releasing this into the education system and revising the way their students are trained to talk, can then reshape their thoughts and opinions of their host society and also give them the ability to destabilize and implode one society after another in a very indirect and subversive way.

When evaluating the literature currently used in Western societies, we don't see it structured to say Brown people, Black people, or Yellow people thousands of times from first to twelfth grade. We don't have class lessons seeking to maximize the number of times we need to use the term Brown people, Black people or Yellow people to complete our writing assignments, classroom conversations, or receive a passing grade. Yet we do see the literature in our public schools structured to say "White people" thousands of times from first to twelfth grade.

We do see classroom lessons maximize how many times students must use "White people" to complete writing assignments and classroom conversations. We see teachers give instructions requiring students to use whiteness or White people in projects to receive a passing grade. We're immersed in literature that doesn't train us to think, speak and write about Black, Brown, and Yellow people the same way it instructs us to think, speak and write about White people. And therefore, they have not used the American student body as a tool to create the same singular record for Black people, Brown people and Yellow people that it has been used to create for White people.

How did these materials become embedded in our public school curricula? If you look closely at the curriculum committee selecting the pool of material used at each school location, you'll find literature structures declaring their intention to center all conversations around White people. This trains the students, who take these classes, to hold generic conversations about White people and refer to their American host population as White people instead of American.

In addition, literature manufactured here in America that creates generic criticism about White people has been circulated through education networks into other Western societies, like Ireland, Germany, and Sweden for use on the host populations there. The children in those schools are not being trained to refer to the Germans as German, the Swedish as Swedish, or the Irish as Irish. The students are being trained to call them all White people instead.

Let's use Sweden as another example. Imagine a radicalized teacher going to the curriculum committee at Sweden's public schools and installing a lesson plan structured to center all conversations and writing assignments around White people. This will train the student population to do several things because it revises how they write, talk, and think.

First, it trains them to stop referring to the host population as Swedish and to start calling them White people. This begins separating the Swedish inhabitants from their own Swedish identity, negating and delegitimizing the existence of the Swedish people. The Swedish identity will no longer be validated or acknowledged in conversations or literature produced from then on. As far as the Swedish identity, it will no longer be attached to the Swedish host population. It will no longer belong to the Swedish people; they'll be known simply as "White people" by the generation coming in behind them. Once it's been severed, the Swedish identity can be used and claimed by other unrelated populations, whether they share Swedish heritage, value or protect it, or choose to publicly attack everything it consists of and work to erase it piece by piece.

Second, it ensures that the children in Sweden's public school system are trained to speak, write, and think, using a language structure that implicates all populations in the same color group. Simultaneously, it incriminates the Swedish host population with every classroom conversation or writing assignment completed about White people. The teacher can also exploit Sweden's student body and use it as a tool to create a giant academic cache about White people. This stockpile will consist of academic papers and projects they can use in other countries, through the education system, and employ it as a weapon against host populations worldwide.

Third, by using a broad color category as a shared identity, the teacher can transfer blame to the Swedish people for things they had nothing to do with. Using a lesson plan that has generic wording about White people means that students in that class would have no way to tell if the events they were being taught about were done by members of their own Swedish host population or a different population from another part of the world. Each time they hear or use "White people" in their writing and classroom discussions, it also incriminates their Swedish host population because they are included in that same color category. It will shape students' opinions toward the predominantly White population hosting them, resulting in the students resenting their host population or becoming radicalized and attacking it.

Finally, as the rhetoric developed inside the classroom spills out onto the streets, prolonged exposure to generic rhetoric about White people will eventually create public resentment of the Swedish host population. Most people exposed to this rhetoric reflexively assumed it was the Swedes being referred to every time they heard "White people this" and "White people that," in school lectures or broadcast via large media platforms.

Eventually, a segment of the population will become radicalized. Some extremist politicians may exploit that public resentment for money and votes by coordinating with splinter groups to carry out "social justice" attacks against the Swedish host population. They will also support attacks on Swedish identity, cultural symbols, traditions, heritage, and eventually their right to be validated and exist as a people. All because of long-term exposure to generic criticism about White people for things that weren't done by the Swedish. This is one method radicalized teachers would use to turn the children in Sweden's school system against their host population, while using them to sabotage it from within. Children can be deceived into thinking they have shared guilt and their population is to blame for random historical events, that they're undeserving of their own society, and now have a responsibility to destroy their country from the inside for the sake of "justice."

Then, after destabilizing and imploding Sweden, that teacher can go to the next country and use the same lesson plan in the schools there. Without even rewording it, as long as the host population of that country falls into the same color category, every time the students are told "White people this" and "White people that," they'll automatically assume it's talking about their own host population. The teacher will turn the children against their own country and induce the psychology that leads to the self-destruction of the host population.

If the host population is different, all the teacher needs to do is change "White" to one of the other three color categories. Training the children and activists to shout "Brown people" at the host population of Mexico, Pakistan or Samoa has the same negative effect on those societies as training students and activists to shout "White people" at the host population of Sweden, Ireland, or America.

In a subversive way, the radicalized teacher can hijack the education platform and the student body and use it for a new purpose. Instead of using it to educate the children and strengthen that society, they use it to sabotage that population from within and implode it. They repurpose education resources and use the student body as a tool to create material and rhetoric for their goals. Sometimes it's a paper circulated through academic channels in schools in other countries or an article broadcast to the public via a prominent media platform. Either way, this material will tumble across the planet and mess with the heads of the host populations who fall into the color category referenced. Activists can force different host populations worldwide to share the blame, whether they were directly involved in the events being criticized or not and use this to extort them.

But it doesn't stop there. As those students and activists eventually enter the workforce, some will obtain jobs within the education system and design their lesson plans using the same language structure, training an even larger portion of the student population to think, speak and write this way. Others will use this language structure to write the scripts used in radio, television, movies, and daily articles broadcast to the general population. Some go on to work for large companies and use this language structure in business agendas and when developing company advertisements. Some enter the legal field and use this to make their arguments more aggressive and increase their chances of winning their case. Some become politicians who use this to structure public remarks about their host population and make extortion demands from their host population.

Watch for this pattern in your everyday life. Pay attention to how often you're referred to by your color by people in the media, teachers, or other students, instead of American, or for those of you in other Western societies, in a way that reinforces your nationality, heritage, and cultural identity. Watch for highly-influential movie stars, comedians, politicians, and journalists who think, speak and write this way and analyze the effect it has on the general population each time they shout "White people this" and "White people that" from a public platform. Once you start evaluating media for this pattern, you'll notice the agenda is in play in a precise and calculated way. It's always directed at the host population or members of the host population but never directed at other inhabitants, who are trained to use it on the host population. That level of precision, over such a long period of time, confirms that this was released into Western societies and used against the host populations on purpose.

How This Subject Came Up in My Discussion with the Dean

In my conversation with the Dean at my school, I pointed out the lesson plans training students to read, write, and think using a structure referring to people by their color. Teachers have been openly teaching and using this structure on campus for many years.

I asked him, "Did it occur to you that, through a long period of exposure to lesson plans using this language structure, students like myself analyzed it and learned something else in the process?"

Remember, it's been pointed inward at the host population one hundred percent of the time and never directed at the other populations, but the pattern is still visible. Nothing stopped me from studying this language structure, how it works, and how to change the application, so I can redirect it to the other populations who've been trained to direct it at mine.

I then discussed with him how the school administration can't control the application of language structures like this one, which is openly taught on campus, because it's public information anyone can use. School administration can't dictate that only one section of the student population can use this language structure to deliver their public remarks, criticism, and writing assignments, but not another, because that's bias. I then informed him that I would be adopting the same language structure for all assignments and communications moving forward. As such, when students or teachers ask me why I'm using Brown people, Black people, and Yellow people in my writing and verbal remarks, I'll explain it's for all of the same reasons they use White people in their writing and comments.

I made it clear that I'd be using the same language structure moving forward and that I'd talk to teachers and other students the exact same way they've been trained to speak to me. It was at this point that I noticed his eyes widen. Aside from having an "ah-ha" moment and recognizing how he'd been trained to think, speak and write this way, he realized that the tables had just turned. One side had lost its grip on something they've directed at my population for a long time. Now, their language structures will be redirected back at them. They'd dropped their weapon, and I'd grabbed it to use in self-defense.

Though I'd succeeded in my conversation with the Dean, I didn't really win anything because in the end, it was just a conversation, not an agreement to make institutional changes. The Dean made no agreement to hire teachers and adopt lesson plans that will maximize the number of times students need to use Brown people, Black people, and Yellow people in our classroom discussions or as a requirement to receive a passing grade on writing assignments.

There was no agreement to ensure that our population achieves the same level of hands-on training. There was no commitment to making my population equally comfortable when using the terms

Brown people, Black people, and Yellow people to deliver public criticism on platforms like the student radio station or articles submitted to the student newspaper. There was no commitment to ensuring the general student body hears the terms Brown people, Black people, and Yellow people broadcast at it the same number of times it's heard White people broadcast at it. There was no commitment to create the same on-campus environment for the other three colors of people that they have created for mine (even though the school publicly advertises a policy of not treating people differently on the basis of color). In the end, there was no commitment made by the Dean to ensure my population receives equal training.

But you know what? We don't have to wait for a commitment from the Dean or for the slow-moving administration to make these changes. Since we determine the language structure that we use in our daily conversations, social media posts, school assignments and articles that we produce, we're going to use the exact same language structure in all communications with them moving forward. This is a much faster way to change things at the individual level, and bias administrators or faculty can't block it.

Student Actions You Can Take Starting Now

Stop using all other identities when speaking and writing, only use Brown people, Black people, and Yellow people for everything. Start speaking and writing about other populations the exact same way they speak and write about ours. Only by directing the same language structure at them can you make the way they've been trained to speak and write about us visible to them. There may be a few exceptions to this when using group identities, which I'll discuss in the coming chapters.

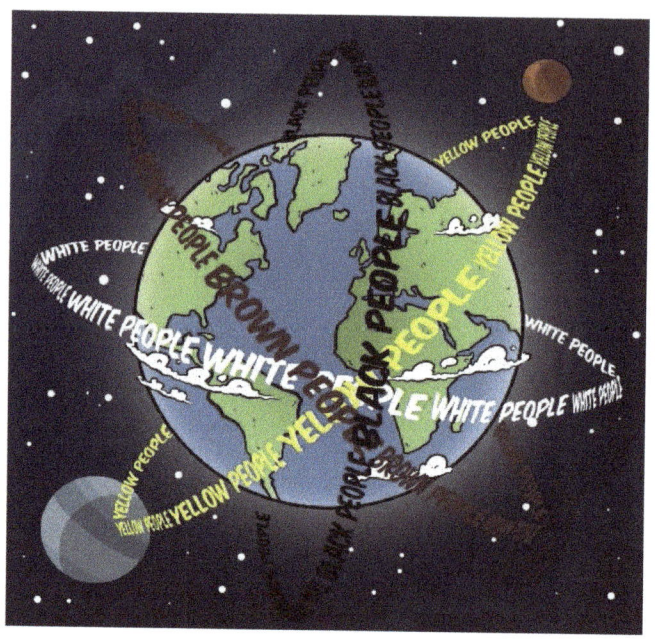

I'd also like you to consider that we've not been trained to use giant movie and news reporting platforms to create and circulate a media cache of equal size and detail for Brown people, Black people, and Yellow people that's been created for White people nor have we produced the same supply of academic literature for Brown, Black, and Yellow people. Right now, the general population is operating under a skewed point of view, which explains why it's always our population who must make concessions to the other populations, but never the reverse.

This all changes and is neutralized once we begin using the same language structure to complete all school assignments, social media posts, daily conversations and media produced. The more of us who adopt this same format each time we speak and write, the sooner we begin the monumental process of creating an academic and media cache of equal size and detail for Brown people, Black people and Yellow people that's already been created for White people. Just think, what are you doing at the individual level to ensure the same number of articles, academic papers and social media posts that mention the other three colors of people circle the globe?

Also, consider how this empowers members of the host population to block future extortion attempts. We have seen activists use this as a shock tactic against ordinary members of the host population who are left speechless when a stranger publicly shouts "White people this" or "White people that" at them from a public platform. It's been particularly one-sided up to this point, and since members of the host population have been denied equal training, they've been set up to lose each time they encounter it. This all changes now, because anything an activist can say about White people, they can also say about Brown, Black, and Yellow people too. Shouting things like this back at them will turn their own language structure upon them and neutralize them.

Separately, I want you to think up disruption tactics you can use when encountering radicalized teachers or activists rambling on about "White people this" and "White people that." Craft a counterargument using the same language structure. Say things like, "So did the other three colors of people..." Or challenge them by asking, "What can you blame White people for that wasn't also done by Brown, Black, and Yellow people?"

When you see activists call something too White, call them out by asking if they also call things too Brown, too Black, or too Yellow. They'll hate that and most of them can't come up with a response. First, it makes the technique they use to structure their extortion argument visible. Second, the response uses the same language structure, which neutralizes the effect they wanted to have. Making this visible will begin to undo the impact it has on the general population.

To illustrate this, I once successfully neutralized a radical professor in front of her entire class. She snapped at me, saying, "Blanket statements about Brown people, Black people, and Yellow people are not fair because they can misplace blame on other innocent populations." I then counterargued that the way she structured her initial remark about White people does the exact same thing, because she is referring to one of the four color groups. The look on her face indicated an "ah-ha moment," and she moved on without responding.

The point is this. I want you to take every opportunity to challenge and educate teachers and other students slowly and carefully. Many teachers, professors, and Deans received their entire education with literature using this format, and it's the only way they know how to write, speak, and think. They may become defensive because it can cause insecurity and rattle the foundations of their beliefs and viewpoints. The main thing is to use their language structure in reverse. All other social effects, the rebalancing of the existing academic and media cache and the deprogramming of the general population, will happen independently on its own.

All you need to do is make sure that whatever you produce lists the person's color when you speak or write. You don't need to be mean, you don't need to be rude or argue with anyone, just make sure the person's color is listed and is part of the permanent record in whatever you create moving forward.

One article, social media post, or school assignment at a time may seem insignificant, but as the saying goes, grains of sand eventually form a heap. The key to neutralizing the existing media cache that's circling the planet is to make sure an equal number of articles, social media posts, and (eventually) movies are circulating the globe. Only then will this structure become visible and lose its effect on the global population. Simple as that.

Shift Blame Using Race

Unlike color identity, which uses physical appearance to determine which color category someone belongs to, race is far broader. It includes people who do not present as White or would not identify as White in a social setting.

The American census defines the White racial category as: A person having origins in any of the original peoples of Europe, the Middle East, or North Africa, including Hispanic and Latino populations. In an over-simplified way, anyone who's not categorized as Black or Asian is classified as White. So instead of grouping people into four categories as discussed in the previous chapter on color, race further consolidates people into three broader categories. The main difference is that there's no category for Brown people, and that population gets split between White and Asian. Now you can imagine how easy it is to trick and confuse members of the public, who base what they think "White" means on the pictures they see it paired with throughout the media. Based on this widespread misunderstanding, let's look at some of the methods used to frame, agitate, and destabilize the host population in America.

How We See This Used by Media

Look at the pattern in the articles broadcast to the public. Let's separate them into two categories: articles that include pictures and those that don't. For pieces using "White" with a picture of the person in question, we are usually shown someone with light Whiter skin and recessive features. If the general public sees a picture like this each time they see "White" in an article or commercial, they'll base what they think White means on the collection of images they see in these articles. But what about articles calling someone White but lacking a picture of whoever they're talking about? In these cases, the piece usually refers to someone without recessive features, who does not resemble the images in the other articles or commercials. However, they're still included in the broad racial category of White by technicality because they do not fall into the Black or Asian racial category.

You'll also see the picture excluded if the person in the article is in a category receiving group-based special treatment by the Government. Whenever the mainstream media broadcasts reports using the term White, but does not include a picture of the person, the general population will automatically assume the media is referring to someone, who looks like the pictures in the other articles which are continually broadcast at them. It's this collection of images that will appear in the mind of the general population as they absorb what media is broadcasting at them. As such, it's the people who resemble that collection of images which the general population will assign blame or resentment to. This will happen each time they encounter articles or media reporting that uses the term White, but does not include a picture of the person it's talking about.

This is one way that large media outlets take the blame for the crimes of special-treatment groups and shift it to other populations the Government doesn't protect. Worse yet, innocent people receive social backlash or in some cases, become victims of revenge attacks.

Does this sound a little confusing? Do you ever wonder why large media outlets refer to someone as Asian or White when they don't look like they would identify that way? Years ago, America passed laws prohibiting the media from reporting in a way that reflects adversely on minorities or other special-treatment groups. These laws pushed for crime statistics and media writing to use descriptions involving broad racial categories instead.

Since these laws now exist, special-treatment groups can employ legal teams to pressure media companies into removing the picture of the person they're reporting on along with other information identifying which population or special-treatment group they belong to and refer to them as White or Asian instead. Unfortunately, the people, who visually resemble "White" or "Asian" in the public mind, receive the blame and backlash for the crimes committed by various special-treatment groups. The special-treatment groups get a sweet deal out of this arrangement.

One example, I recall an example that gained national media coverage. Two people got into an altercation and one shot and killed the other. For the first week, the media bombarded the general populace with continuous media coverage and articles referring to the shooter as White but did not include a picture. When random people decided to carry out revenge attacks or went into the streets to get "racial justice," they went looking for people who resembled that collection of pictures they saw in past articles or commercials, and which were paired with the term White. They hunted down people, who resembled those pictures, and who they thought the media was talking about each time they broadcast the word White on everyone's television, social media, and radio 24/7.

About a week later, a picture of the shooter surfaced, confusing the general public because the shooter didn't look White. He didn't look like all the people who had revenge attacks carried out against them. Then we saw the large media outlets stop referring to him as White and start referring to him by hyphenating the word White onto his special-treatment group identity. This may have been the first time most Americans saw large media platforms use White identity in this hyphenated way. Of course, this was after a week's worth of nationwide revenge attacks had already done irreparable damage to a different population.

Let's evaluate what the mainstream media did when reporting this story. An accurate way to describe what happened is to say that one minority shot and killed another minority, yet who did the media blame? White people.

The person the media referred to with their collective hysteria was a member of two different special-treatment groups, each with their own identity and officially recognized by the federal government. The press could have described the shooter using either group identifier to avoid transferring retaliation and blame to a different population. And yet, supposedly independent, large-scale media outlets used the same scripting and referred to him as White. We witnessed large-scale media platforms work together, read from the same script, withhold the shooter's picture, and omit any details that would identify which special-treatment groups he belongs to.

They did all this while repeatedly referring to him as White, on a national scale for an extended period. At the same time, countless revenge attacks and acts of domestic terrorism occurred against innocent members of a different population who were not involved in the shooting.

These media platforms coordinated to cause destabilization and used this technique to get minority populations to carry out revenge attacks against the host population from the comfort of their fancy offices. In addition, we saw politicians exploit this tragedy by using the same deceptive language in their political statements, both past and present.

This situation highlights the resentment expressed by the host populations of various Western societies. These larger populations have been forced to host special-treatment groups without their consent. The media and political platforms use tactics like these to inspire special-treatment groups to carry out revenge attacks against the host population. In the host population's view, certain special-treatment groups have exploited loopholes in the media and crime reporting systems.

Some groups use this cover as a blank check to behave as badly as they please and commit as much crime and trouble as they like. They know they can have the blame for their bad deeds shifted back around to the population being forced to host them. The result is that there won't be a criminal record of each special-treatment group's bad deeds. The ability to block a record of their crimes from being created and then to shift the blame for their crimes to another population was all achieved by lobbying to have crimes reported under the broad racial category that's shared with the other populations. So, instead of reporting their crimes under the specific group identifier that the federal government uses to officially recognize them as a people, and which gives them continuous special protections and special treatment, these crimes become reassigned to another population, most often the host population.

Whenever the media uses White without showing a picture of who they're referring to, it's often because that person isn't visibly White. If the media uses a photo or indicates to which special-treatment group they belong, their story won't create social backlash or cause revenge attacks against the population the press wants to target. The media uses this tactic to shift blame for crimes committed by people who do not identify or present as White in public, to those who do.

Since most existing laws and media company policies are only structured to protect special-treatment groups but leave most of the White population unprotected, there's currently no legal recourse to stop activists and media companies from using this tactic as a domestic weapon and a means of destabilization. The one-sided reporting and censorship we see in the media will continue until the laws are changed, and the remainder of the White population possesses the same legal recourse and protections under our own government that the special-treatment groups were given long ago.

Let's Analyze How This Tactic Is Used in Academia

I once watched a woman who identified as Brown during her introduction give a PowerPoint presentation comparing nationwide crime statistics by race. One of the slides she referenced showed the total crimes Whites committed being substantially higher than the crimes Blacks and Asians committed.

She used the disparity to frame the White population as problematic. Then, this Brown woman carried on about "White people this" and "the White race that," for the remainder of her lecture, while the audience remained silent and let her finish. I could tell this was not what her audience expected when they agreed to attend a talk about race and crime. What was the real purpose of this presentation? Let's look closer and determine the real purpose by analyzing what she did.

First, we have a woman identifying as Brown. By doing so, she separated herself from the White racial category about which she made her remarks. Then she went on to frame Whites as disproportionately violent compared to the other racial categories listed on her slide.

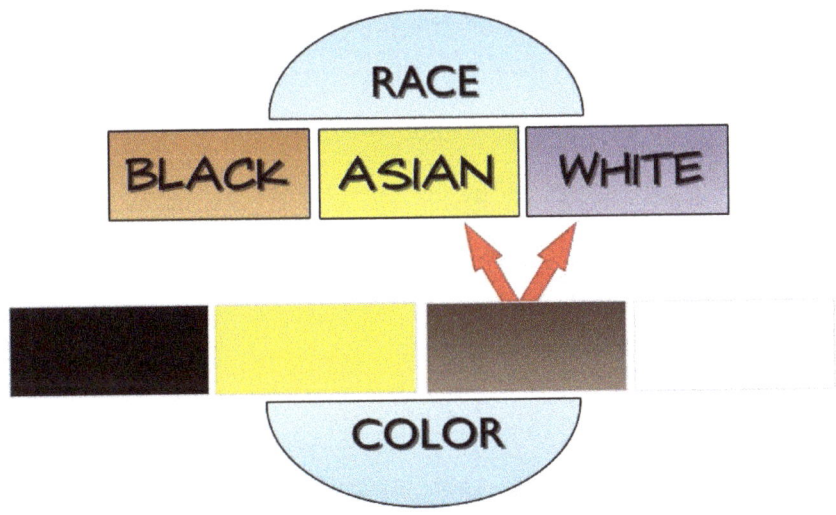

To reiterate, there is no category for crimes committed by Brown people or people who identify as Brown. Crimes are registered by racial classification, not color. All crimes committed by Brown people, who look like the woman giving the presentation, are recorded as committed by either Whites or Asians. Therefore, Whites and Asians receive the blame for all the crimes committed by Brown people.

This woman went on a public stage, citing crime statistics inflated by her own population, and used those inflated stats to put White people on trial. She made prosecutorial arguments about White people to frame that population as problematic, all while distancing herself from the White category by identifying as Brown. Once I noticed this, I realized this was no innocent mistake or oversight. This woman had training and knew exactly what she was doing. Labeling her presentation as a study of race and crime was just a way to camouflage a presentation meant to shame, shock, and agitate a different population by exploiting this technicality. This was nothing more than a public shaming session directed at White people.

There are multiple subgroups for the White racial category in the crime statistics academics often cite. The crimes these subgroups commit are recorded in a different category than crimes committed against those same groups. All the crimes that White racial subgroups commit are recorded as crimes committed by Whites, while crimes committed against these subgroups are filtered out and counted separately in a special category. This has created a one-sided criminal record for each of these subgroups. There is no record of the bad deeds each subgroup commits. These crimes and misdeeds have been hidden by shifting the blame to Whites while all the bad things done to these subgroups have been filtered out, counted separately, and can be maximized when constructing group victimhood narratives in academia.

Anyone can give an academic presentation using numbers that hide the negative things done by a particular subgroup, while increasing the focus on bad things done to that subgroup and skew the audience's perception, all without disclosing what they're doing.

You may notice that members of special-treatment groups initiate most publicly staged conversations about race and crime. Public discussions about race and crime automatically tilt in their favor, because there's no historical or criminal record of negative actions taken by their specific group, just of bad things done to their group. You'll also notice that representatives for multiple subgroups use this method to form their collective victim narratives and publicly call for their fellows to unite against White people.

I'd be willing to bet that if we change criminal reporting to create a separate collective record of the crimes committed by each of these subgroups, you'd see these staged conversations on race and crime quickly disappear. Instead of putting White people on trial for crimes committed by these subgroups, they'd be putting their own subgroup on trial and forced to publicly own the collective bad deeds of their subgroups. The technicality they use to transfer blame for their group's ill deeds to White people would then be disabled.

Consider How Activists Exploit This Loophole

People who engage in this behavior as a form of personal activism or to deceive the general population, are people I refer to as "part-time Whites." Part of the time, they call themselves White and part of the time they use their other group identity (the one they're protective of).

This is an excellent formula for evaluating subversive activists who flip between different identities: When they do good, they identify as "X"—and when they do bad, they identify as White. Using this tactic to shift blame for the crimes of their group to the White population and then using those inflated crime stats to put the White population on trial, is encouraged as a form of activism by radical subversive subgroups.

One pattern to watch for with people who use multiple group identities is to find the one they protect. This will identify what they truly consider themselves to be. That's what motivates their actions and activism. It's that group identity you see them spend money on or lobby for special treatment on behalf of. When they want special treatment, it's only for their specific subgroup and never for the broader White identity that they hop in and out of, and use to transfer blame for all their bad deeds to.

Consider How Academic Radicals Exploit These Tactics

We see many academic programs and fields of study based on group identity marketed to the student population. Imagine if the students in these classes weren't told that the crime stats they're being shown about Whites were actually all crimes committed by their own subgroup population. Think about how long-term exposure to lesson plans or other academic literature focused on crimes committed by Whites can be used to radicalize and recruit from those subgroups who become resentful of Whites. A radical teacher can recruit activists from various subgroups, using crime statistics inflated by those very subgroups without letting them know that. This can take place because the literature referenced by the radical teacher is written as though these are crimes committed by Whites, and none of them would think to look for this technicality. That is, that the crime statistics are actually from the subgroups the activists are recruited from.

Even though it's misleading, academics get away with this ploy because the subgroups who committed those crimes are classified in the White racial category. Deceptive and misleading? Yes. Illegal? No, and for the radicals who make these tricky or circular arguments, it doesn't really matter, especially if they believe the ends justify the means. There are no laws to stop them from using this tactic in future lesson plans.

Fast forward a generation and consider how they'll word lesson plans to teach about the 9/11 attacks. Radical teachers can remove any pictures of the attackers from the lessons and word their syllabus to refer to them as White because that's the broad racial category the attackers fall into. It's not illegal, there's no law anyone can use to block such an agenda. For radical academics who want to destroy Whites and whiteness, it's one more tool in their toolbox, one more dirty trick to play on the host population, and one more weapon against the next generation.

So, how do we put a stop to this type of deception? What can we do to derail such a plan? We need to demand formal subgroup recognition by the federal government.

The Need for Unique Recognition

When evaluating the need for unique recognition or discussing the complex problems caused by being denied recognition, there are multiple layers to consider. Currently, our population is contained in one large, shared-identity category with multiple different subgroups. The other subgroups each have a separate, formally recognized subgroup identity that they are protective of. However, our population is left without a unique identifier.

Not only are we the only remaining portion of this broad racial category left unrecognized, but we've also been left unprotected by our own government. The result is that the other subgroups have used the broad "shared identity" as a dumping ground and a means of having the blame for their crimes and bad deeds transferred over to our population. Social blame and resentment is transferred to whomever the broader society thinks "White" means, each time it's used to refer to the crimes committed by the other subgroups.

Activist members of other subgroups devise creative ways to sabotage our population. This results in attacks carried out against us. One common tactic is making duplicitous statements of "we White people this," and "we White people that," knowing it will cause public backlash and revenge attacks to be carried out.

They could just as easily present themselves using their other group identity (the one they're protective of) but that would redirect the public backlash and revenge attacks back at their own subgroup instead of tricking the general population into carrying out attacks against a different population. So, they don't. They use this duplicitous way of speaking as an indirect way for their subgroup to carry out tribally motivated attacks against our population. It's an indirect form of warfare. They know that it's the people who look White or are considered White in the minds of the general population that will be targeted for retaliation and revenge attacks. *Think of it like a folded lie.*

Their own subgroup will be unaffected because they can easily disassociate by using their other group identity. They don't present as White in person and have a secondary subgroup identity they guard closely, so they don't care about the one they share with our population. They can vandalize, disparage, and entirely destroy the group identity they share with us, along with our entire population using this tactic. And they'll be fine, because their other formally recognized identity, the one they're protective of, the one that receives special treatment and legal protections, will not be destroyed in the process.

How do we disable such deception? Simple, we must have a formally acknowledged unique subgroup identifier. We must demand our government give us the same official recognition they've already given to every other population contained in the broader racial category. We can no longer remain the only part of the White racial category left unrecognized. As long as the only population-based identity we have is one that's shared with other subgroups, who are trained to resent us and who use it to sabotage us, they'll keep using the shared identity as a dumping ground, and as a tool to cause continuous harm to our population.

We live in times where different parts of the population take revenge based on what they're taught in school and shown on TV. As long as the word White is being thrown around in the education system and on media platforms, we must demand that our own government give us the tools to fix this. Only by establishing unique recognition and changing the law to report all crime by subgroup can we stop this type of subversion and sabotage.

A Few Other Variables to Consider

Currently, we cannot accurately measure our access to schools, scholarships, jobs, and other opportunities. A large university can publish a pie chart showing the student body is twenty-five percent White, but we have no way to measure distribution among the subgroups that this percentage may include. Besides, tribal loyalties can easily come into play when one subgroup works as a team to deny access to other subgroups within an institution.

What about situations where different subgroups ally based on their collective victim narratives and work together to deny access to our population or anyone they assume is White? We've been left without a way to measure our level of access as a group. Imagine how different those Ivy League pie charts would look if they were required to post each subgroup and what percentage of the student body or staff each subgroup comprises.

Consider the mainstream conversations we've experienced regarding wealth and wealth redistribution. Have we been blamed or penalized for the wealth of another subgroup? (Yes.) We've seen policies and legislation structured to punish and disadvantage our specific population justified using conversations on White wealth without measuring the distribution among each subgroup in that category. For all we know, one subgroup may be starving.

In contrast, another subgroup may have an overabundance, or one subgroup can team up and economically choke out another. We have no way to measure that if we are denied a unique identifier. Since discussions on wealth and wealth redistribution play a role in politics and conversations on equity, the measurements need to be accurate. We need to ensure we're not penalized based on a different group's wealth.

We have no way to measure discrimination or compile the data and evidence required to seek justice through the established legal system. We can't do that if we have no unique identifier and remain unrecognized. This makes it impossible to compare the percentage of our access to institutions, to the portion of the population we compose. If other groups work together to "bottleneck" us or deny us proportionate access to our own institutions, there's no way to document it if we're denied a unique identifier. Denying us a unique identifier is a creative way to block our access to seek justice through the legal system.

We must disable the deception and blame-shifting tactics currently used in academia and by the media, especially since we can see how they've used this as a weapon against our population. Radicalized professors, who already refer to other subgroups as "White" to generate backlash against our population will continue to do so, as long as we are denied a unique identifier. Large media outlets will continue to do this as well. We must also secure self-representation at all levels of our society and institutions. We've already seen tribal loyalties override equal protection under the law and lead to various forms of sabotage.

Our population needs more control over how the media portrays us. Do you ever wonder why our population gets so much backlash from movies and media articles? If we're not in charge of any movie studios or MSM networks, we don't have a say in how stories are framed or worded. Ask yourself, who are the people organizing this, and what is their motivation to continuously produce media that causes attacks on our population?

Protection and Legal Recourse

As the law stands now, when tribally-motivated attacks between different subgroups occur, some get in trouble for it, but not others. The laws don't stop the favored groups from carrying out such attacks against other groups, so these laws need to be updated and any loopholes closed. This double standard is a source of frustration and tension between different populations in the same broad racial category. There is an entire legal caste system that exists inside of this one broad racial category that's not being addressed. Self-representation in the legal field is essential because most attorneys specialize in "Minority case law," which is a different legal framework that doesn't include established precedent for our population. If you go to one of them for representation, most of the time they'll say they can't help you.

We Must Demand Re-enfranchisement

Policies or laws outlawing "White" organizations usually have a "minority exception" built into them. So, even though it was made illegal for the "White" population to organize, it's not unlawful to organize based on subgroup identity. Only our populations were disenfranchised by these policies, since we had no subgroup identifier. Other populations with subgroup recognition have been able to organize this entire time. That's why we have Hispanic, Jewish, and Middle Eastern groups on campus, who are not outlawed from organizing even though they are also included in the same White racial category we are. Only our population is prohibited because we lack the same formally recognized subgroup identity every other population possesses.

Consider this. Los Angeles will lose funding in some of the public schools that are "too White," while some of their schools are one-hundred percent Hispanic. If Hispanic is one of the subgroups in the "White racial category," why aren't these schools losing funding? Because there is a "minority exception" built into our laws. All the other formally recognized subgroups can have their own organizations and their own communities. It's only our population who was disenfranchised by being denied subgroup recognition because the only population-based identity we are left with was outlawed by this type of legislation.

Laws passed at the state level seek to ensure populations are represented by members of their own group. Still, our population gets disqualified by laws at the federal level that outlaw White organizations. This, combined with other laws at the state level, results in every other population getting political self-representation except ours. With laws like this being passed at the state level, it's time for the federal government to repeal the laws they used to disenfranchise our population.

So, What Subgroup Identifier Do I Propose?

I like the term White-Ethnics for several reasons. It's plural and acknowledges our shared ancestry without erasing our different heritages and ethnic identities. It also has reclaiming properties when we pair it with other heritage-based identities. I understand that further discussions will be necessary amongst the populations this impacts and possibly some disagreement on which name to use. But the primary purpose is to establish a unique identifier for the reasons this chapter outlines and not to delay by arguing about what words to use. We can always revise that down the road, but based on our immediate needs, we need a formally recognized identifier the other subgroups do not share or hop in and out of.

We need what the other subgroups in the White racial category have had this whole time. We live in times when rhetoric is used as a weapon to sabotage and frame our population, and establishing unique recognition is the only way to disable that.

The American census already acknowledges people having origins in any of the original peoples of Europe, but denies a unique identifier like White-Ethnics.

A Working Definition for White-Ethnics

- The only remaining portion of the White racial category who is left without a recognized subgroup identity.

- We are not coded as Minority in the legal system so we are already separated out from the other populations and acknowledged as a different people at the government level.

- We live and operate in a different legal framework than the other subgroups do.

- We are the portion of the population that the government has left unprotected.

- We are not acknowledged as being Diverse.

- It is not categorized as racist to deny us access to jobs or admission to our own schools because of who we are. And it's not considered a Hate Crime to attack members of our population, our identity, way of life, culture, symbols or our right to exist collectively as a people.

- We know ourselves to be the original peoples of Europe.
- We know ourselves to be the founders of the American nation state.

Student Action

What other criteria would you add to the list? What other traits define someone as a White-Ethnic?

Consider using the term White-Ethnic in your writings and social media posts. That will begin laying the foundation we need to establish formal recognition. When you catch the media or teacher referring to someone as White remember to dig a little deeper and find out which subgroup they're referring to. Who did you think it was referring to initially? Then, after researching to find which subgroup it is, compare that to who it wound up being. Consider the differences you find and if the remarks or lesson plan used by the teacher was intentionally structured this way to shift blame or be deceptive.

Call attention to any books and media you see produced by part-time Whites, claiming to speak on behalf of all White people. Analyze people who use multiple group identities. Write out all of the different identities they use, and circle the one that they're protective of (that's the one they consider their true identity and that's what motivates them to do the things that they do).

Political Action—Consider the Following

Present direct questions to your local politician and lawmakers. If they won't support passing legislation at the State or Federal level to stop the use of these tactics, then ask what they're going to give us to defend our population from the negative effects that are caused by them.

Reach out to your local politicians and communicate to them that we want formal subgroup recognition established. See if you can find out how the process works and what steps need to be completed in order to get the legislation process started in your area.

Present direct questions to any politicians who resist giving us formal recognition. Ask them, why wouldn't they want us to have formal subgroup recognition and disable the tactics used against us? As well, why won't they give us the ability to measure our level of access to schools and institutions and an ability to evaluate them for discrimination against us?

Publicly confront people who use multiple group identities. Point out how they say or do things that damage White identity but they don't do the same things to the other group identity they use. Why do they only spend money or push legislation to protect one group identity but not the other? If they use both identities, why would they trash one or leave one unprotected, but not the other? This is effective when analyzing people who are active in identity politics and use multiple different group identities. Research and find out which group identity they're protective of and which ones they don't care about. Look for that pattern to see which one they are protective of and which one they allow to be openly attacked and remain silent while that occurs. This'll tell you what they truly consider themselves to be and what motivates their actions.

I call them part-time Whites. Have you thought of something more effective to call them?

Antiwhite Media and Literature

My understanding of antiwhite literature and rhetoric is this: Users structure it to use the word White in a negative way, the maximum number of times possible. They use it in a way that assigns baggage and negative meaning to it or in a way that programs their audience to feel hatred toward the word "White." They take the word White and attack it, shift blame to it, torture it, curse it, vandalize it, and disrespect it, knowing that every population linked to the word White will also be slandered and hated in this process.

Most of the people promoting antiwhite viewpoints consider themselves to be social engineers and they know that a population of people cannot exist unless their group-based identity is officially recognized and validated socially. That said, if you analyze radicals who say things like whiteness must be destroyed or White people should not exist, you'll see their goal quite clearly.

The goal in destroying a recognized population of people and slowly revising them out of existence, is to first destroy their group identity and ensure it's no longer officially recognized, socially validated or reinforced by the general population.

This is because any population, which does not have an officially recognized identity, will no longer exist as a group, and will be mixed away into a sea of global traffic.

These radicals look for ways to turn the word White into a liability and discourage the population from reinforcing its existence or claiming it. That's why we see specific media platforms produce a steady stream of articles about unimportant and stupid topics that nobody seems to care about. The stories themselves are not the real point of these articles. This endless stream of posts is just used as a vehicle to ensure the general population sees the word White used in a negative way and as many times as possible.

And, if the author can't refer to a person as White, you'll see them refer to the car, someone's hair, or someone's shirt as White. The media creates articles about local events that don't matter to anyone but have the word White packed into them, perhaps ten to twenty times. They do this to ensure the word White will be stored in the mind of the general population, along with a collection of negative stories and events that they have seen the media attach to the word White.

You'll see agitators on TV posing as news anchors or unfunny comedians. Often, it seems like what they're talking about doesn't matter to anyone. They're just trying to see how many times they can say the word White in a negative way, on a public platform. Ask yourself, what are the most times you've seen the word White packed into an article, used by a media reporter, or placed in a so-called comedy skit? I've seen the word White up to fifteen times, packed into a four-paragraph article.

Manipulate Language by Flipping Between Race and Color

Activists use different definitions and framing structures to attach the topic discussed to the word White. Let's consider a few of these.

Uses in Media

What techniques do you see the media and academia use to maximize the number of times they can negatively use the word White and attach hostile sentiment to it? When studying the tactics used by large media companies, it seems more about how many times they can pack the word White into an article and less about the topic itself.

Since the media, which is broadcast to the general population on a daily basis, is reported from many different angles, you'll notice different authors or media personalities will use different definitions and different framing structures each time, in order to shift blame or attach the discussion topic to the word White.

We see media maximize the number of times they can use the word White by flipping back and forth between using the broader definition of race versus referring to someone by their color or visual appearance. For those so-called journalists, who want to abolish whiteness or White existence, it's about using the word White in a way that harms it each time they speak or write. It's about choosing between the definition of race or color and selecting the one that enables them to use the word White in whatever they're working on at that moment. Stretching the definition as far as they can and making it as elastic as possible is a means of shifting blame from other groups and building the biggest and most negative record surrounding the word White.

Then they use that exaggerated record as a weapon, to put White people or whiteness on trial in the court of public opinion via large media platforms. Reviewing a history of articles written by the same author will reveal how they have bounced back-and-forth between the techniques discussed in the chapter on color or the chapter on race to maximize the number of times they can use the word White. This process creates the narrative they need to get the general population to react the way they want, towards anyone perceived to be White.

Watch for this pattern in media reporting. If they include a picture of the person they're reporting on, does that person look White? If they do, then they can refer to them as White because that's what color they are, and it's supported by their visual appearance.

If that person does not appear White based on their color or visual appearance, then we commonly see media attempt to lighten the photo or completely remove the picture of the person they're reporting about because they're using the broader racial definition of White that includes all people, who are not in the racial categories of Black or Asian. This enables them to still use the word White in a negative way and shift blame to it, whenever reporting on the deeds of people who don't look White and who the general population knows by a different group identity.

Next time you see a media story with a White focus, question the author's motive. Is this story really newsworthy or just a piece of antiwhite literature? How many times did it use the word White and was it positive or negative? Did the author use it in the context of color or race? Does the author use a consistent definition of the word White in their past works, or do they bounce back-and-forth each time to attach the discussion topic to the word White? Consider the role fiction writers play and how they use their stories as a vehicle to vandalize the word White. Whether fiction or not, it still installs the same negative perception into the mind of the general population. Analyzing media this way will reveal specific patterns along with the author's true motive.

Methods Used in Academia

Antiwhite academics use similar methods to maximize the number of times they can use the word White or pack the term "White people" into their literature and lesson plans. For instance, look at teachers, who lead classes that are marketed directly to minority groups. They use the tactic discussed in the chapter on race. They take all the crimes committed by minorities inside the White racial category and change the wording to refer to the crimes committed by those minority groups as crimes committed by White people. Since most of the students in these classes claim a different group identity, they're unaware that the crimes committed by their own population are registered as crimes committed by White people. I have seen this deception tactic used as a tool to radicalize and recruit foot soldiers from those classes for activism and other purposes.

Look at sensitive subjects, like slavery and consider this. If the academics who designed the lesson plans used in American schools referred to slave traders and slave owners by their color, ethnicity, tribal, or current minority-group identity, they couldn't call all of them White. So, what did these so-called academics do? They used the broader racial definition of White instead, which enabled them to use the word White in a negative way and transfer blame for slavery away from those different subgroups and over to whoever the general population thinks White means every time they saw it used.

It also explains the use of cropped slave narratives (more on this later). On a larger scale, we see that antiwhite literature and lesson plans are used in the classes that are marketed directly to minority groups, which means antiwhite ideology and resentment is the common thread that connects all of these different groups mentally. And this is what's used to unite them against, what they perceive to be, White people or whiteness.

Think about this logically. If you're going to group populations together on the basis of race or color, then there's nothing you can blame one color category or racial category for, that the other color categories or racial categories can't be blamed for as well.

There's not one thing you can blame White people for that Brown, Black, and Yellow people haven't also done. There's not one thing you can blame on the White racial category that you can't also blame on the Black and Asian racial categories. Out of the four color categories, each population can be grouped together by their color and put "on trial." Out of the three racial categories, each population can be grouped together by the racial category they're in and put "on trial." A pattern you will notice is teachers are unwilling to use literature or make remarks about Brown people, Black people, and Yellow people that they make about White people. They're not willing to use literature or make remarks about the Black or Asian racial category they make about the White racial category. When you encounter a teacher who does this, ask yourself:

Why would the teacher use literature or structure their remarks to group people together by racial category or by color category when they refer to Whites but not use this exact same literature and language structure when referring to the other populations? Why would the teacher use literature or structure their remarks to put White people on trial for things that are not unique to White people? What's their real intention?

It's simple. Instead of using the academic platform for education purposes, they use tunnel vision or a limited focus to put White people on trial for things that are not unique to White people, so they can attack the whole White population.

Antiwhite teachers use the word White in a negative or derogatory way the greatest number of times possible. They flip back and forth between using it in the context of color to the context of race and create lesson plans and discussion topics requiring students to use the term White in a negative way, as often as possible.

In addition, they promote a belief system to unite other populations by framing White people as their common enemy. In order to put White people on trial for things that aren't unique to White people. Narrow focus, also known as limited scope, is used to structure their remarks or lesson plans in a way that leaves their students thinking the topic at hand is something that's unique to White people, when it's not.

They redact any reference to other populations to make students think that whatever topic or subject they focus on is unique to White people. The teacher is not condemning a specific topic or issue; they are just looking for different angles to attack White people from. This approach is highly effective because their audience won't realize something is missing unless someone else points it out.

One common example of this is race-based income comparisons. White people are not the highest earning group, but White people are the target during these discussions. Public income comparisons don't compare the income differences between all populations; they redact the groups at the top of the list. Like the cropped slave narratives or the privilege checklists, this is another creative angle they use to attack White people and justify legislation or policies structured to disadvantage and harm the White host population.

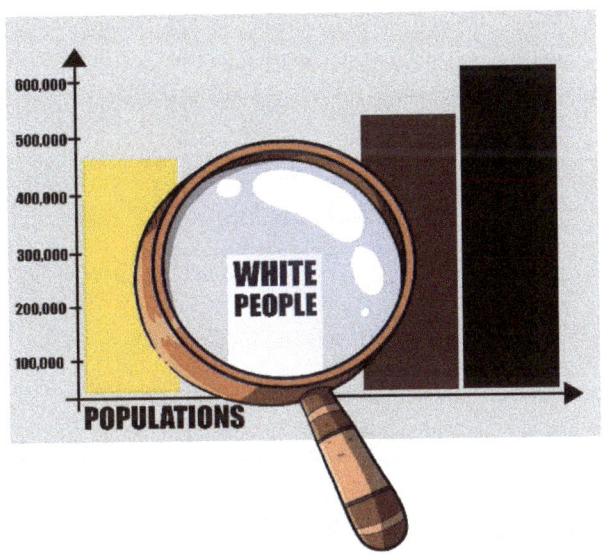

Does it seem like an attorney putting your population on trial wrote these media articles and school lesson plans? Well, some of them were designed by radicalized attorneys. We see them putting White existence or the White population on trial using the alternative wording "whiteness" to avoid direct liability or accountability.

Other methods used in antiwhite literature or by antiwhite teachers include erasing the historical accomplishments of White populations. These teachers also delegitimize White existence by incrementally banning their cultural elements. They find ways to hold White cultural symbols and norms to standards that they don't hold any of the other populations to, so they can just ban those of the White populations. To do this, they use unpublished criteria for terms like "offensive."

Let's use flags as an example. This tactic works because if a school had to publish the criteria that determine if a flag is considered "offensive," it's likely that other flags would meet that criteria and they'd have to ban all flags. The only way to ban our flag and no other is using secret criteria, so no one can apply them to other flags the same way it's applied to ours. The same goes for cultural symbolism, holidays, religious practices, social norms, etc.

Another pattern to notice is that activists only have something to say when White citizens defend themselves and they remain silent during attacks on White citizens. When they police the way people talk to one another, they're very one-sided about it. High-powered leagues and legal organizations also behave like this. When evaluating institutions like these, use their historical pattern of performance to confirm their true intent. Analyze when they appear or have something to say, and when they remain silent, while attacks get carried out. That pattern will confirm if they are antiwhite.

Student Action

Practice identifying antiwhite teachers and literature and challenge them.

Consider how many academic hours you have been exposed to antiwhite literature. Think back to the earliest years, what is the earliest grade level you remember encountering this type of literature or rhetoric. Consider the social conditioning that happened by being exposed to this literature year-after-year, as you made your way through the school system. Also consider how the other populations have been conditioned as well. And along with this, consider all of the negative social effects caused by long-term use of antiwhite literature in our own public school system.

Think of ways to disrupt it and delegitimize it. Analyze the methods you see used by these radicalized teachers, audit the things they say and the literature they use. Disrupt the teachers, who use this rhetoric on campus. As well, pick their methods apart and break down any material used by them. Any member of the White population has the right to audit anything that uses the word White in a way that shifts blame to it, assigns baggage to it, or makes others resent it. We have this right because of the negative social effects it causes for our population. When you hear the teacher use the term "White" or say "White people," ask them to clarify their definition.

Are they using the definition of color that references someone's physical appearance? Or are they using the broader racial definition of White, which conceals the color or ethnic identity of other groups who don't look White in person? Ask why they're calling them White instead of being more specific. Use direct questioning and put the teacher on the spot.

Consider which population the students think the teacher is referring to when they say "White people." Is that the same population the discussion topic is actually about? It's essential to make the teachers clarify this, particularly if their lesson uses deceptive wording to conceal a person's color or ethnic identity by calling them White instead of the other group identity the general population knows them by. If they try to shift blame to our population for something we didn't do, then these types of corrections and interruptions will neutralize their agenda and make it malfunction. It also makes the deception visible to the rest of the students in the classroom.

For Literature

Deconstruct antiwhite literature and audit it every time you encounter it. Start by determining which definition of White the author uses. Do they refer to someone by their color and visible appearance, or do they conceal their color and ethnic identity using the broader racial definition of White? Then analyze the social effects this literature has on the general population to determine the real motive of the person who wrote and distributed it. The academics who design the school curriculum, structure their remarks and literature in order to create the social atmosphere and effects they want to see. It's not an accident when you locate literature that uses these methods, they do it intentionally to engineer a specific outcome.

Look for more than just someone who uses the word White. Do they use the word White in a way that assigns baggage to it, vandalizes it, or shifts blame to it? When you see them use the word

White, call them out and confront them. Criticize the literature, criticize the author, criticize their manipulative use of the word White, and criticize the teacher for using our public education platform to distribute it. As you analyze, ask yourself:

1. Does this literature create positive or negative social effects?

2. Is this piece of literature something that will agitate the general population and cause resentment, backlash, riots, or revenge attacks?

3. If the author referred to the group or individual in their article by their color, ethnic or tribal identity instead of calling them White, would this change...as a result...which group received the public resentment, backlash or revenge attacks?

4. Did the author shift blame from one population to another by referring to them as White instead of using the color, ethnic, tribal, or minority group identity the general population knows them by?

5. If the author knew there was a strong chance their material would cause public backlash or revenge attacks, why wouldn't the author avoid misplaced blame by being more specific and referring to people by their color, ethnic, tribal, or minority group identity instead of White?

6. If the author could word their literature to avoid redirecting backlash to a different population, yet deliberately chose not to, what's the author's real motive?

You see, if the author had the option to word their literature in a way that would not redirect backlash to a different population, but deliberately chose not to, then what's the real intention of the author? What is the real reason they chose to word their literature the way that they did and then release it into the general population?

This gives you the ability to determine the authors true motive by analyzing the way they structured their material. You don't need to ask the author to explain themselves, or give them the opportunity to lie to you. You can simply analyze the alternative wording options they had available to them, along with the social effects caused by the material they released into the general population, and use that information to determine their true motive on your own. You have the ability to audit them and all of the material they produce. You can point out how wording things differently would have had a different effect on the general population or redirected blame and backlash somewhere else. You can call out the tactics they used and publicly criticize them for what they have done along with any damages they have caused.

For example, when I analyze an article or piece of literature that causes social problems, I ask myself, could the author have avoided misplaced blame by being more specific and referring to whomever their article is about by their color, ethnic or tribal identity? If so, and they chose to refer to them as White instead, to redirect public backlash and revenge attacks over to a different population, then I know that the author did it on purpose. It's a hit piece. If you don't like a specific population and want to incite other groups to carry out attacks against them, you can use tactics like these to write your articles and distribute them using large media or academic platforms.

I want you to become good at this type of analysis and include it in your activism. Consider the alternative wording options the author had available and the different social outcomes that would have had. Then, render your decision on their motive. Once you are good at this analysis, you can turn the tables on the author. You can take a hit piece that they wrote, turn their literature into a liability, and use their work as a piece of evidence to put the author "on trial" in the court of public opinion.

Charge the person with deliberately causing trouble. Tell them, "You had the option to word this differently. You chose not to do it and purposely caused trouble for my population!" Lift the curtain so other people can see who manipulated them through deceptive language. Remember, these radicals have many names to call everyone else and are very touchy about every word and term that's directed at their own population. They knew exactly what they were doing when they sought to use the word White in a way that would cause problems. This tactic is deliberate and calculated, keep that in mind when you publicly charge them. Then deliver that charge via a large and highly-visible public platform.

Political Action

Consider that a lot of the political organizations and politicians that we see in the mainstream media formed their viewpoints, while going through a school system that uses these tactics to format the lesson plans. Without knowing what tactics were used on them or recognizing that they were delivered using language manipulation, their worldview is skewed and they don't even fully realize it. That said, these are the people writing policies and laws who were taught to consider it a form of justice to block our access to our own institutions and systemically disadvantage our population.

Challenging this type of agenda requires political involvement. I want you to become involved locally and think of ultimatums you can present to any local politician asking White citizens to vote for them. Explain to them that we don't want to go to schools that have this type of material embedded in their curriculum. Further, we don't want our communities to be within the striking distance of the other populations that have been trained to attack us.

Also, consider disrupting and withdrawing all support from politicians who make, or who have made, antiwhite statements in the past. You can easily point out that any politician who really wanted to see multiculturalism succeed would not make antiwhite statements from public platforms and cause perpetual social problems.

Only support political representatives who take the public position that antiwhites are not welcome in America, or any other Western society for that matter. Only support political representatives, who commit to banning the use of antiwhite rhetoric and material in any taxpayer funded institution along with repealing any existing policies and laws that are antiwhite in nature.

Cropped Narratives

Are you familiar with the concept of cropping a photo? You know, cutting off the parts that you don't like, or cutting out certain details that you don't want other people to know about before you present it to the public? You'll notice this same concept used with highly sensitive topics that have been taught to us in our schools and broadcast at us from public media platforms for decades now. Take traumatic historical events as an example. The general population can be put under the impression that a certain historical event was the only one of its kind simply by cropping out all of the other similar historical events from any school lesson plans or media. The same can be done with historic atrocities. The general population can be put under the impression that one population is uniquely guilty of a certain atrocity simply by cropping out all of the other populations who did the same thing, from any school lesson plans or mainstream media reporting. To bring attention to this tactic, when I see narratives like this used, I call them out by referring to them as "cropped narratives," as a way of making the redactions and editing visible to others. Let's take the topic of slavery, for example.

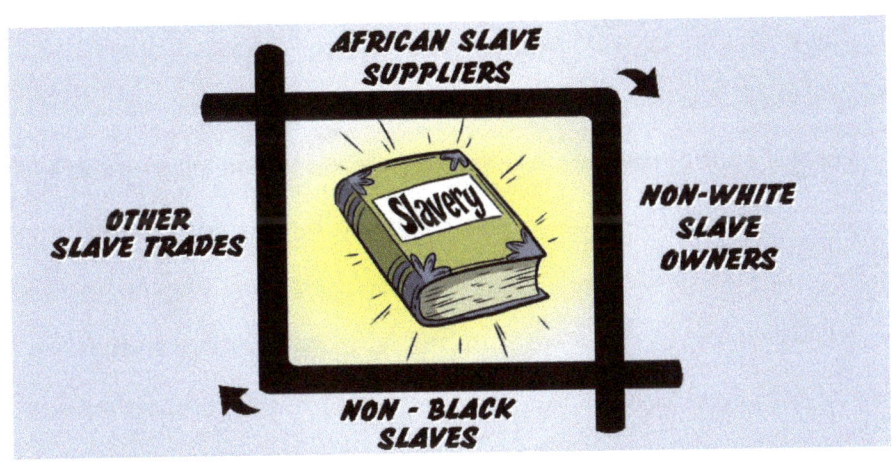

Academia

If we analyze patterns in the material we see used in the school system. We will find that the pictures and illustrations shown will almost always portray the slave owner as appearing White, and the slave as appearing Black. We see this same pattern when analyzing the collection of stories selected. The slave owners are referred to as being White and the slaves are referred to as being Black. Historical illustrations or stories of slave owners who were not White, and slaves who were not Black, have been cropped out of the standard lesson plans.

Since the collection of illustrations shown to students always presents the slave owner as being White and the slave as being Black, and the collection of stories selected always refers to the slave owner as being White and the slave as being Black, the students who have this collection of cropped narratives shown to them are put under the impression that only White people owned slaves and only Black people were slaves.

We notice that the lesson plans use words like kidnapped to leave students thinking someone who was foreign to Africa, journeyed there and snatched up a Black slave by surprise. Instead of using words like exported to leave students with the impression that it was Black Africans, who made their money by trapping other Black people and selling them off as slaves to the rest of the world. We will find plenty of pictures and illustrations of people who purchased slaves being portrayed as White. But any pictures or illustrations of non-White people who trapped and supplied the slaves to the rest of the world, have been cropped out of the standard lesson plans.

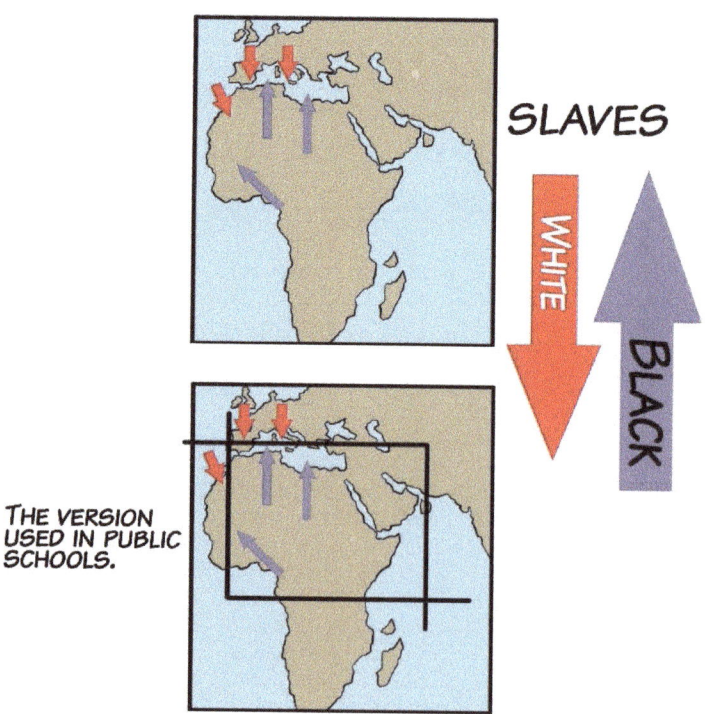

SLAVES

WHITE

BLACK

THE VERSION USED IN PUBLIC SCHOOLS.

Or as discussed in the previous chapter on antiwhite literature, the academics who decided the way the lesson plans on slavery would be worded, decided not to refer to slave traders and owners by their color, ethnicity, tribal or minority group identity. They decided to call them all White instead. This way, they could transfer blame for slavery away from those different populations, who the general population currently knows by a different group identity, and over to whomever the general population thinks White means every time they see it used.

When we analyze the tactics used in academia, we see more than one layer of deception built into the standard lesson plans. We see deceptive wording used to mask other well-known populations involved in slave trading by calling them White instead of by their color, ethnicity or current minority group identity. And we see slave owners, who could not be called White as well as slaves who were non-Black, cropped out of the lesson plans.

Whether it is coordinated by the high-level academics who are designing the standard lesson plans that will be used at multiple school locations, or through selective editing done by the curriculum committee at each school, you can see how cropped narratives are used to control what students think about the practice of slavery. They're also used to direct where the students will assign blame for slavery, who they will demand concessions from, and who they will carry out revenge attacks against.

Media

We see similar patterns used in the media that is broadcast to the general population.

Repetition is one key tactic used to keep the concept of slavery fresh in the minds of the general population. This is achieved by continuously producing miniseries, TV shows and even large-scale movie productions that always portray the slave as being Black and the slave owner as White. Any ethnic sounding names, cultural clothing or symbols that would identify a specific ethnicity, tribal or minority group identity are cropped out as a way of controlling where public blame is directed, for whatever program they're broadcasting at the time. In situations where you do see ethnic sounding names, clothing or symbols of other populations being amplified, it's usually for the character cast as the Black slaves "ally." You know, to encourage solidarity against White people.

Now, for those of us who do historical research, we will find that the population portrayed as an ally to the Black slave, usually played a leading role in the transporting and selling of Black slaves to the rest of the world. As such, it would be more accurate to cast them as the slave owner instead of the slave ally. But, since the majority of the general population doesn't research or audit the media, which is broadcast at them to see if it's accurate, movies like this are successful at achieving what they're intended to do. The goal is to dictate the role each population played in the slave trade, and control where the general population assigns blame for slavery and who they consider their ally in the fight against slavery.

One interesting pattern you will notice among these top media and movie producers, is that they never portray a member of their own tribe as the slave owner. Think it's because they know the movie or media they're producing will create social backlash and they don't want it to be directed back at their own group? Why else would this pattern exist? After decades of these cropped slave narratives being publicly broadcast, just imagine what's been installed in the collective mind of the general population.

Wealthy People and Politicians

Aside from what we see marketed by media and academia, we see this collection of cropped narratives receive further support from wealthy donors, as well as from subversive politicians.

We see wealthy globalists pay to restore old locations or resurrect old buildings where the slave owner can be referred to as White, while ignoring all other locations and buildings where the slave owner cannot be referred to as White. We see politicians use the same tactic using taxpayer money to erect monuments, establish history centers or museums, where the slave owners can be portrayed as White, and the slaves portrayed as Black.

This way, the general population will only see a standing collection of historical centers, monuments and buildings where the slave owners are all portrayed as White, and slaves are all portrayed as Black. Everything else is ignored and cropped out. This carefully constructed collection of buildings, monuments and historical centers are used to provide additional support to the impression that all slave owners were White, and all slaves were Black. An impression which was originally installed in the mind of the general population using the cropped slave narratives circulated in academia and broadcast by media.

In addition, we see politicians and activists in other countries exploit this mirage that's been constructed in America. This is a way of making the cropped slave narratives they use in another country appear more legitimate. We usually see the politician or activist deliver a performance via a large public platform intended to catch the population by surprise and put it into a state of shock. This performance is immediately followed up with extortion demands, such as demanding financial concessions, reparations or the introduction of aggressive laws and legislation written long before they delivered their performance. Ambushing the host population this way and putting it into a state of shock, increases their chance at passing group-based special treatment laws that exclude the host population or laws that can be used as a weapon against the host population and continuously steal from it.

Social Effects

Consider some of the negative social effects this has on the general population. In White societies, we see this mirage used as a form of psychological warfare against the White population and as a tool to wound it and make it malleable using psychological guilt. We see this used to justify the passing of laws or policies that harm the White host population and steal from it in the name of "atonement" or "racial justice." But on a global scale, we see it used to agitate Black populations and use them as a tool to create mass destabilization, violence and destruction.

Consider how the long-term use of these cropped narratives and the mirage that's been built on them, have been used to radicalize the Black population and incite them to carry out revenge attacks on complete strangers. There are multiple cases where random White people are hunted down or attacked by someone they don't even know. As a justification, the person who attacked them makes comments or a reference that it's revenge for slavery. It's only through the use of cropped slave narratives that a person can be incited to carry out revenge attacks on a complete stranger. Of course, the justification is based on something that the attackers own population is guilty of doing too.

It's only by cropping it out of the collection of stories that are constantly shown to them, and keeping that information from them, can you make someone feel uniquely harmed and entitled to take revenge on another population, for something that their own population did too. If the pictures and illustrations of people who look like the attacker, or the role that the attackers population played in the trapping and selling of slaves all got cropped back into the collection of slave stories they were shown in school, I'm willing to bet that they would not be radicalized. And as a result, they would no longer feel inspired to carry out revenge attacks on the members of another population, and the Black populations around the world would not wind up being used as a tool for destabilization and destruction.

Let's take a broader and more general look at the use of cropped narratives and the social effects they have on the general population. Slavery is not the only sensitive subject we see being used for this purpose. Let's say we have someone like an academic or someone who is wealthy that engages in social engineering, on their own. If they wanted to make the population of an entire country malleable and make it accept certain conditions which would be rejected under normal circumstances, we see the use of cropped narratives designed to inflict psychological guilt, as one way to achieve that. These cropped narratives are tightly controlled and broadcast at the general population continuously over a long period of time. They are slipped into the media stream and presented as a one-on-one media interview or an opinion piece article, but it's always done in a way that the narrative can't be challenged. And no reference can be made to any of the information that they cropped out.

As this collection of cropped narratives is broadcast at the general population over a long period of time, without the general population having the ability to challenge them in an equally visible way, they're eventually accepted. The result is a sense of guilt is successfully assigned to the population there. Once that's done, we see them install a guilt monument or some sort of symbolism of the guilt that they've assigned to the host population. The guilt monument or other symbol then serves as a constant reminder and something that can be used against the host population continuously. We also see legislation and other concession demands made to harm that host population and to extract resources from it and transfer the resources to a different country or to a different group in the name of atonement or reparations. Of course, none of that would be made possible and the host population of that country would not allow itself to be looted, if all of the information that was cropped out of those narratives, got cropped back in.

Regardless of who the group is that's using cropped narratives to make extortion demands, anyone who looks back far enough into the history of that specific group, will find a time where that group is guilty of doing all the same things they're demanding compensation and reparations for. It's only by cropping this information out of the narrative they use, and keeping this knowledge hidden from the general population, that they can present themselves as uniquely harmed, deserving of compensation, special treatment laws and convince other populations to join them and unite in their effort to attack the host population that they're pointing their cropped narratives at.

With so much on the line, this is why we see these cropped narratives so tightly controlled. We have even seen politicians in other countries make it illegal to investigate certain cropped narratives or attempt to show the general population any of the information that's been cropped out. The use of cropped narratives is a very valuable tool for politicians and elites who use this tactic for social engineering purposes. Broadcasting cropped narratives can be used to get an entire city burned down, agitate and destabilize an entire society and implement group-based redistribution policies and programs that continuously steal from one population and redistribute to another.

Taking these details into consideration, consider the following. Do you think the use of cropped narratives and the construction of guilt monuments randomly happened on its own or do you think this is something that was preplanned?

I think this seems preplanned. Think about it. If the use of these tactics was not planned or was not coordinated, then we would see some inconsistencies in the way they're applied, and the way social blame is shifted. You will notice the use of these tactics is never directed back at the various special treatment groups, who direct it at the host population. Since we don't see these inconsistencies in the way they're used, that gives us enough information to know that the use of these tactics is coordinated and planned in advance.

Do you think this is something that will go away on its own if you ignore it?

I don't think this is something that will go away on its own because there are too many people who have found ways to benefit from it. Consider rich people who own stock in jails and the many companies that service the jail populations. They make money off the violence these tactics create and all of the people who wind up going to jail as a result of their violence. Think of all the politicians and activists who make money off of group-based extortion operations. Think of politicians who have dual citizenship and use these tactics to have legislation passed that takes money or other resources from America and transfers it to the other country they have citizenship in. Think the other country sets aside some money for them in a bank account over there each time they do that? There are various other populations who run media outlets or movie studios, who make a living by producing and circulating cropped narratives that frame the White host population and continuously aggravate other populations. And there are those who simply enjoy using public platforms to carry out attacks on the White population. So, I don't see this going away on its own simply by ignoring it.

Student Action

At the student level, you can call out material being used by teachers by asking direct questions. Instead of focusing on the narrative itself, change the focus to the design of the narrative and the intention of the author. Ask them things like, what social effects are they trying to cause by cropping out all of the non-White slave owners and non-Black slaves from our lesson plans?

Write a request to those who design the lesson plans and ask tough questions. For example, what social effect are they looking to cause by calling the slave owners White instead of referring to them by the ethnic, tribal or minority group identity that the general population currently knows them by?

Or ask them if they're willing to revise future lesson plans on slavery to include illustrations and stories of non-Black slaves and non-White slave owners. Will they consider referring to the slave owners they do include by their ethnic, tribal or minority-group identity, instead of just calling them all White? Make their answer publicly visible for other people to see.

- Request the school library to offer books about Non-White slave owners and non-Black slaves.
- Publicly label lesson plans or other narratives as being "cropped" as a way of making how they have been edited more visible to others.
- Investigate which teachers or education officials coordinate the use of cropped narratives inside of the

education system and think of creative ways you can disrupt them.

- Analyze the existing monuments or historical centers in your area.

Ask yourself, were there other events like these that happened in the past that have been cropped out to make the public think these were the only event of their kind? Consider which groups benefit from the monument. Ask yourself, have the bad deeds of that group been made visible so the public can see them and know about them too? Do you think these groups would still obtain public sympathy if their bad deeds were made visible to the public, or would they be considered a worse group, who should be making concessions to other populations?

Evaluate other countries where you see a guilt narrative assigned to the host population using certain symbolism or a center that was established to be used as a guilt monument. Call them out, stop supporting the population that created these guilt monuments and work to have these monuments removed. Consider writing the manager of these sites to crop certain information back into their narratives and displays. If they say no, do you suppose they want it to remain the same so they can continue using it to guilt and extort the host population? Consider who benefits and who is harmed. What cropped narratives do you see directed at your own population and what are they used for? Are they being used to demand fee stuff?

What are the most common cropped narratives and guilt monuments you see used in each country?

Political Action

In my opinion, cropped slave narratives and cropped narratives in general have been used as a multigenerational weapon. They have been used as a tool for large scale extortion, harm and destruction. Take an inventory of politicians (possibly with dual citizenship) who have used cropped narratives to pass legislation or make extractions from America and transfer it to another country. Stop all support for them. The Government must take steps to balance out what's been installed in to the mind of the general population by the long-term use of cropped narratives. Do not provide support to any politician unless they negotiate with schools in their district to revise the lesson plans on slavery or any other cropped narratives used in that region. They must work to balance out the collection of taxpayer funded buildings, monuments and historical centers that reference slavery to include non-White people, who owned slaves and non-Black people who were slaves in America. As well as ensuring they accurately list the ethnic, tribal or minority group identity of slave owners instead of concealing it and shifting blame to a different population by calling all of them White, instead. Also, they must make themselves available and work with local students and constituents to report cases where they see any of these tactics being used and work on ways or present legislation that will deter their use as well as require schools to use lesson plans that crop non-White slave owners and non-Black slaves back into the standard lesson plans.

Social Prosecution

Have you ever heard of putting someone or a group of people "on trial" in the court of public opinion? This concept is what I refer to as *social prosecution*. This is when we see someone take the same tactics attorneys use to prosecute someone inside of a courtroom, and use those tactics outside of the courtroom, in the public sphere. They use the large public platforms provided by academia or media to deliver their prosecutorial argument and put other people or entire populations "on trial," in a publicly visible way. They charge them with crimes and prosecute them the same way in a social setting, as an individual would be prosecuted inside of a courtroom.

Academia

In academia, we see how antiwhite material is used to connect multiple different groups by the same ideological string and unite them against the White population. We see how these different groups have been trained to encircle the White population and read from a script that's been compiled over a long period of time, to put the White population on trial in the court of public opinion. From multiple different angles, public platforms are used to lay charges against the White population and make aggressive demands for concessions or justify theft, vandalism and violence.

Whether it be from the angle of sexuality, color, race, religion, tribe or anything else they can construct, what all of these special studies programs have in common is that they all use material or literature that's pointed at the White population, or White people in general. Year-after-year, large volumes of students are steered into these special studies programs that train them to put the White population on trial from that specific angle. By using this structure for all assignments and discussions the students receive long-term, hands-on training as they make their way through the education system. It's by long-term exposure to arguments that charge the White population with crimes and no exposure to anything that would contradict those accusations, that the White population gets incriminated in the eyes of the students, who go through these special studies programs. In these programs they can be convinced to feel justified doing anything that they're recruited to do at a later date.

Consider the students who read from the script that was marketed to them in class or who follow the instruction they're given in one of these special studies programs. Ask yourself, do you think the other populations involved are fully aware of the social role that's been designed for them to play? Do you think these students or their parents fully understand what purpose these radicalized teachers are using the students for?

Effect on the General Population

Let's consider this from a social engineering standpoint and analyze the effect it can have on the general population of an entire country. In order to put the host population on trial and nobody else, a public platform is given to various groups to deliver their prosecutorial arguments and accusations. However, an equally visible platform is denied to the host population to repeal the charges that are publicly levied against it. From multiple angles, these different groups are trained to encircle the host population and use public platforms to deliver their prosecutorial arguments and charges against the host population. At the same time, they are also making aggressive demands for concessions, or justifying violence and destruction of the host population.

By allowing the host population to be charged with crimes over a long period of time and ensuring they have no platform to deliver their defense, or the ability to confront their accusers, they are falsely incriminated. The result is that they are viewed as guilty in the eyes of the public. These charges become even more believable when used over a multigenerational period as the younger generation have only heard the accusations made by the various other groups on public platforms. They have not heard the defense arguments made by the host population. So, without firsthand knowledge of the events that took place before they were born, the only thing they are left to believe is that the host population is guilty of all crimes the special treatment groups have charged it with.

This false sense of guilt will make the host population become malleable. Members of the host population can be pressured to compensate on a personal level by giving away their opportunities and possessions to their accusers in an attempt to prove their innocence. They can be pressured to forfeit access to their own institutions and submit to legislation or policies banning their own holidays and social norms. This will incrementally destroy them, their population, their society, and their entire way of life.

Additional steps are taken to fortify the use of these tactics so they can be used to extort the host population on a long-term basis. Various special treatment groups work to pass laws used to charge members of the host population with hate speech if they defend themselves verbally and hate crime if they defend themselves physically.

Consider the position this puts the host population in from a social engineering standpoint or when making changes to an entire society without their consent. All of the laws on the books are one-sided. They are structured to offer zero protection to the host population. They make it illegal for the host population to publicly criticize any of the other groups who charge the host population with crimes. The other groups themselves have zero restrictions on their own behavior. Further, they are trained to charge the host population with crimes using public platforms and make group-based extortion demands. The host population finds itself encircled by public platforms used to put it on trial on behalf of other groups. These groups are not made to stand trial themselves and are most likely guilty of all the same things they accuse the host population of. See what's been set up here?

The host population is set up to be completely gutted and various one-sided protection laws make it illegal to fight back. Consider that whoever chooses the collection of stories or narratives that are used in the school curriculum and broadcast on public media platforms, is choosing which groups are put on trial and which groups get a free pass for historical and current actions. If there is a long-term pattern where it's only the host population put on trial and never any of the other groups, then this gives us enough information to know that this is being done by design and coordinated. This pattern would not occur naturally on its own. It only happens with someone controlling it and making it happen in a one-sided way.

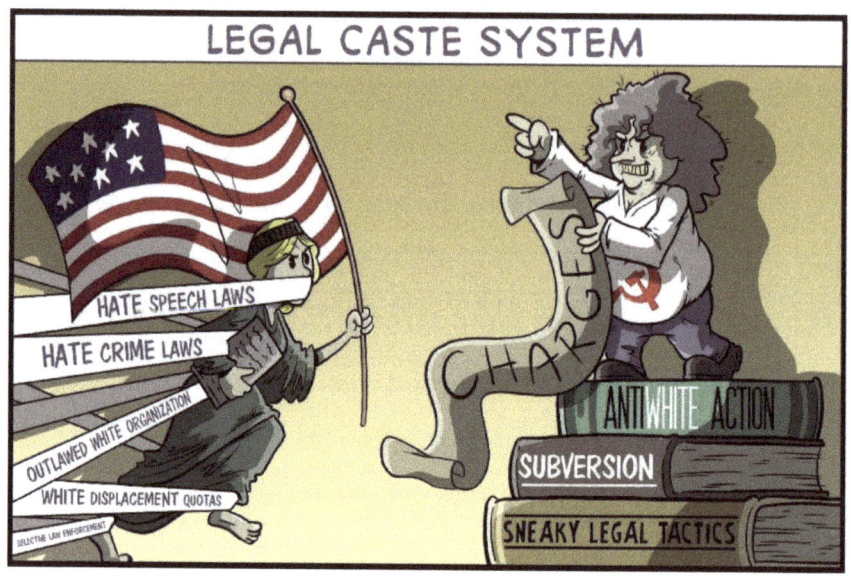

Who Would Support Using This Tactic?

Different people support the use of this tactic for different reasons. Consider the billionaire oligarchs who want to bring about globalism without the consent of every existing society on the planet. They'll pay to train groups to use this tactic because when paired with politicians who have group-based redistribution legislation on stand-by, it steals everything from the host population and redistributes it to the other groups, who were trained to encircle and attack the host population. It's a way of dissolving an existing nation into globalism without the need to change the laws or obtain their consent.

Or consider communists who want to bring about their global communist government. Using these tactics to install a sense of guilt on the host population, along with passing laws to steal from it in the name of reparations or racial-equity, is a way to repurpose the government infrastructure into a giant redistribution system. The holidays, cultural norms and traditions can then all be banned for being "offensive" to the special treatment groups. Soon the entire society can be dissolved into globalism. The host population will be completely looted. Everything will be extracted and transferred to the other groups who were trained to encircle the host population and read from the scripts that charge it with crimes while demanding concessions.

Student Action

Consider that, using social prosecution tactics to harm and loot a host population only works if the host population is denied access to the records of the historic crimes committed by those various groups. And, at the same time, denied a public platform that can be used to defend itself from the charges levied by those groups. This only works if the public displays remain one-sided and are only used against the host population to make extractions from it. If you think about it logically, it's not like the host population did something that the other groups didn't also do. It's just that they haven't had public platforms used to charge their groups with crimes and put them on trial the same way that they do to the host population. These public platforms and these accusations enable them to set up an *extractionary environment*. By portraying themselves as uniquely harmed, they become entitled to make extortion demands. So, think of ways to cause their agenda to malfunction.

Ask yourself, are you being put "on trial" on behalf of groups that have not been made to stand trial themselves? If so, would the other groups deserve compensation or concessions from our group if their collective deeds are worse than ours?

Analyze their argument. Are they using the language structures we discussed in the previous chapters on color or race? If so, we don't know who owes concessions to who, until they are grouped together by color category or racial category and put on trial to determine which group is worse than the others. I mean, what charges can they levy against White people that can't also be levied against Brown people, Black people and Yellow people, right? The only reason these other populations feel entitled to make demands of you or talk down to you is because they have not yet been grouped together on the basis of their color, race or tribe and made to stand trial in the court of public opinion. The only reason it appears justified for them to put our population on trial is because the existing academic and media cache has been one-sided this entire time.

Special treatment groups view your population as being lower than theirs. This is because the material used in schools is not structured to put their group on trial. And the standard lesson plans are not focused on the past crimes of their group. The result? They feel this false sense of entitlement to attack our population and cause harm to it.

Think of it this way, if two parties are arguing a case in the court of public opinion, and one is trained to use aggressive language while the other is required to use submissive language, then one of them has been set up to lose. If one side has been trained to construct arguments that put an entire racial category or color category on trial, but the other side has been denied equal training along with the information they need to put the accusers racial category or color category on trial, then this sets one side up to lose. The one side will lose because they have not received equal training in how to construct counter arguments that will carry an equal weight.

Special treatment groups didn't go to schools where the literature or collection of narratives was structured to group them together by color category, racial category or tribal identity and put them on trial. They don't have media platforms that are solely dedicated to reporting the crimes of their group or broadcasting media at them on a daily basis that's structured to lay charges against their group. Everything they base their sense of entitlement and arguments on is invalid because this tactic has been used on one population but not the others. Once this academic and media cache is evened out and contains an equal volume of material that groups them together and puts them on trial it will remove their sense of entitlement and neutralize their extortion demands.

The problem is you've not been trained to use the same prosecutorial language when speaking to the other groups or when speaking about them. Using group-based prosecutorial language each time you write an article or make a social media post, will have the same effect as putting them on trial in the court of public opinion. This use of prosecutorial language will equalize the social atmosphere.

Look at the guilt monuments and guilt narratives that have been used as a multigenerational weapon against other countries like Germany. Stop participating in rigged public forums. Do not provide any support or validate any demands for reparations, concessions or racial equity transfers. These terms are nothing more than alternative wording used to camouflage race-based theft and redistribution policies. These redistribution policies are enriching other groups whose collective bad deeds are not also being presented to the public. If you don't redirect their arguments and demands back at them, you're participating in a one-sided extortion agenda that's used to steal from the host population and redistribute those stolen goods to special treatment groups who are not being made to stand trial themselves. It's no accident that the laws are structured to offer zero protection to the host population, or that they're trying to ban our only current form of self-defense, Your First Amendment: Freedom of Speech.

White Privilege

Before getting into the White Privilege argument, I would like to point out that it's the criteria that's put on a privilege checklist, which will determine who that privilege checklist is going to be pointed at. A privilege checklist can be created and pointed at any one or at any group, simply by changing the criteria that's put on the list. Thus, whenever I encounter these preplanned public discussions on privilege, I see them as nothing more than a public shaming exercise or a public humiliation ritual. These are very similar to the public shaming sessions that have been used in past communist movements.

Whenever I encounter one of these discussions on privilege, I analyze it from a social engineering standpoint. Things I take into consideration would be the groups involved in the discussion, who the privilege checklist is being pointed at, who's doing the pointing, what criteria had to be listed and what criteria had to be left off in order to control who it will be pointed at, and so on. Every time I see these discussions taking place, I realize they are nothing more than an activity that's used to publicly shame the host population and to make it submissive to various special treatment groups. After all, if they wanted to have a generic conversation about the concept of unearned privileges, they could easily structure it that way and include all groups, but that's not the true reason for these sessions.

That said, when analyzing the material that's passed out or any criteria originated by those participating in the exercise, I recognize two main interpretations of privilege directed at members of the host population.

One interpretation is used when referencing the ability to pass. This interpretation is used by people who remove or conceal certain ethnic or cultural symbolism along with other identifiers to change their appearance and present themselves as a member of the host population. Blending in this way makes them feel like a member of the host population instead of an outsider. It makes them feel entitled to the host population's way of life, along with the collection of rights and freedoms of that population. Using this interpretation, it would be accurate to say the person passing has "privilege," as they do not possess the same inherent rights that true members of the host population have. They would not feel this sense of belonging or be able to publicly project a sense of entitlement, if the host population were to know that they have a higher loyalty to a different tribe. And if ever forced to choose, they would abandon the host populations way of life, freedoms and rights before ever fighting to protect them or before making comparable sacrifices to ensure that way of life, freedoms and rights are preserved. Because they are not truly a member of the host population, I have seen them refer to their ability to pass as having privilege, instead of just calling it passing.

Another thing I noticed is that a lot of the people who promote the White privilege discussions, are part-time Whites and they never promote public conversations or make privilege checklists for their other group identity (the one they're protective of). Also, there is an additional intersection, as some of those subgroups in the broader White racial category are also classified as a minority by the federal definition that's used in the legal system. According to this classification, they could just as easily promote public conversations or make checklists on minority privilege but they never do. Interesting how they sabotage one of the group identities they use but not the other. Makes one wonder what their real motive is.

Another interpretation is used to revise the name of the host populations sense of ownership and rights, which it has to its own society and institutions, by calling them privileges instead. Changing the name enables the sense of ownership and rights of the host population to be delegitimized and publicly challenged by special treatment groups. This is the most common interpretation I see used and is promoted by rich globalists partnering with communists who use special treatment groups to destabilize a society from the inside.

If you think about the way the world exists today, it consists of many different nations and societies. The host populations within each of these feel they have a sense of belonging and ownership to their own society and institutions that other unrelated populations all around the world do not have. Simply put, the unrelated populations around the world didn't inherit what the host population did. They do not possess the same inherent rights to the societies or institutions of other populations, that the children of its founders have. In other words, populations all around the world each have their own.

Now, for those who want to dissolve all of these different societies and nations and just have one giant global system, they need to take away the sense of ownership and rights that each population has to its own society and institutions. To achieve this end, material is produced and circulated that tells the host population that the sense of rights and ownership which it feels it has in its own society, is called "privilege." Further, unrelated populations from around the world are going to be installed and instructed to challenge this sense of privilege.

For those who engage in social engineering, this is the real purpose for these public discussions on privilege. Unrelated populations or various special treatment groups are either provided with the "privilege criteria" lists or are instructed to create lists which contain criteria that any member of the host population would consider to be the sense of ownership or rights they have in their own society. Then, one-by-one, these items are read off and called privileges as a way to strip away the sense of ownership and rights the host populations have to their own society.

Eventually, this conditions them to be submissive to these various unrelated populations and special treatment groups. Even though, criteria can be easily added to these privilege checklists that would point them back at these various groups, and make these conversations work both ways, it's never done. This is not meant to be a two-way street. They are not meant to be criticized back, as this is only meant to be a public shaming session or public humiliation ritual directed at the host population. These various groups holding the public shaming sessions are groups, who lack inherent rights to that society and its institutions. Their goal is to have the host population and its society dissolved and redistributed to them.

For a moment, imagine if I took a plane to Pakistan, went on a public platform there and read from this script telling the people there that the sense of ownership or inherent rights they feel they have to their own society is called Brown privilege. And I'm here to challenge that. Or, as another example, what if I took a plane to Nigeria and read from the same script telling the population there that they don't really have more of a right to that society or the institutions than I do, they just have a sense of Black privilege that needs to be challenged. See how this works?

You'll notice that the items listed on the White privilege checklist exist in all societies around the world and are not uniquely White. They're universal because they exist in non-White societies as well. Thus, it's inaccurate to refer to this concept or sense of ownership as being White, when in actuality, it's universal. There's nothing White about the general concept of inherent rights that all populations have to their own societies and institutions. It's a universal understanding that the unrelated populations around the world do not possess the same inherent rights or sense of ownership to the societies or institutions of other populations, that the children of its founders have. Nothing explicitly White about that. This seems like nothing more than a semantic argument to trick the host population of each society into surrendering their sense of ownership to unrelated populations. These unrelated populations, who played no role in the founding of that society and have as their goal to displace and usurp the host population.

This linguistic trickery is effective as average citizens reflexively defend themselves by arguing they do not possess the unearned privileges on the checklist, when in fact they do possess them. It's just that they're not called a privilege, these are actually the host population's inherent rights.

We see support for the use of this agenda provided by multiple different sources. For those who want globalism, this is one way they use the weight of unrelated populations to leverage out the host population and dissolve a society or nation without its consent. Globalist billionaires who want to dissolve the borders of all existing countries, support the use of this material and tactics like public shaming as ways to achieve globalism without having to change the laws or fight physical wars. You will notice financial support provided to certain colleges and organizations who produce and circulate this material, as well as payments to social media influencers to repeat this scripting from their platforms and work to legitimize it. You will see this supported by communists who want all of the different nations and different identities dissolved into a global communist government. And you will also see these tactics used by lower-level individuals who get personal enjoyment out of being subversive and finding creative ways to menace other people.

That said, there is more than one layer of deception built into the White privilege argument. I see it used as a public shaming ritual and I see the names of our rights being changed to privileges. I see a concept that's not unique to White societies being called White instead of being acknowledged as universal. I also see other populations talk about passing in a way that's intended to confuse anyone who's listening to them. Now, whenever I encounter these discussions or I am expected to participate in them, I like to think up direct questions that I know will cause their public shaming session to malfunction; I'll catch them by surprise.

Here are a few examples.

- Ask if they can explain the difference, between the inherent rights that White people have to their own societies or institutions, and this privilege that they're telling unrelated populations to challenge.

- What precautions are they taking to make sure White people's rights are not being challenged by other people, who are under the impression that they're challenging privilege?

- What can they show you to prove they're not simply changing the name of White rights to White privilege?

- Why aren't they making similar privilege checklists for other populations or special treatment groups? Remember, you can point a privilege checklist at anyone, just change the criteria that's put on the list.

- Or, if the teacher is doing a "privilege walk exercise," ask them if you can add some criteria to the list that tells people to take a step forward. Remember, whomever decides what criteria is on that list, is the one to decide which part of the population is publicly shamed and which part of the population is given a free pass.

Consider the example below.

Take the legal definition of "minority," for example. The legal definition of minority is a fixed, biological definition that does not change or update as the general population changes. It was used to set up a second parallel legal system and special treatment class system which is made up using thousands of laws passed at the state and federal level. These laws only offer protection to populations categorized as minority and exclude equal protection to White-Ethnics. All of these laws combine to make a *legal caste system* that always works in the favor of minorities. These laws have a wide range. They are used to block mild criticism and media that reflects adversely on minority populations as well as require various forms of special treatment. Now, consider all of the material and media directed at White-Ethnics by academia, large media platforms and activists. Think of all the things they do and say to White-Ethnics, which they don't do or say to minorities. Then, construct a privilege checklist out of that. Here are a few examples.

Minority Privilege Means:

1.   Schools won't teach about the crimes committed by my ancestors or tell me that I must atone for them.

2.   The role my population played in the trapping, selling and owning of slaves will be cropped out of all school lesson plans and not discussed in media, news articles or movies about slavery.

3.   I'm given a free pass to say and do things that the host population cannot.

4.   I can depend on receiving a higher level of sympathy from large media outlets.

5.   I am the beneficiary of affirmative action and diversity quota policies that steal opportunities and resources from the host population and redistribute them to me and my group.

6.   I can access and benefit from a society and institutions that my population is not the founder of.

7.   Policies are in place to ensure the interests of my group will be overrepresented in media, social institutions and politics.

8.   Minority privilege is the reason why no colleges or universities require students to complete coursework on, or acknowledge the existence of, minority privilege in order to receive a passing grade and graduate.

As you can see, making a privilege checklist is easy, right? When you think about it, radicals making the argument that "whiteness" is a system can make the same argument about "minorityness." It, too, can be considered a separate operating system constructed using thousands of one-sided protection laws and special treatment policies at the state and federal level.

And for those of you who simply don't want to engage in wild debate with radicals or get involved, you can opt out by stating the following: I'm not in agreement with changing the name of White rights to White privilege. Further, I don't want to be pressured to legitimize revising the name, or speaking this concept into existence through mandatory participation. I will not consider participating in these sorts of discussions until the people leading them can adequately explain how they're differentiating between the inherent rights that White people have to their own societies and institutions, and this privilege that they're telling unrelated populations from all over the world to challenge. And as simple as that sounds, when you do this, the conversation is over.

Denial of Identity

The more I analyze the material used in schools the more I notice that with each passing year, there is an increase in the amount of material that's reworded so it no longer refers to me, or my population as American. Everything else seems to be referred to as American though. There are all sorts of new and exotic combinations that hyphenate American on to just about anything these days. People who are not even legal citizens and have no ancestral link to American heritage are referred to as American, but the population who originated the American identity is not.

Just think, the American identity which was originated by my ancestors and intended to be an identifier of my culture, heritage, and population is being denied to me and my entire population because of the way the literature has been reworded and the inside out way the schools are training people to use it. Once I noticed this pattern, I began to wonder who would want to reword our academic literature so that we are no longer referred to as American and what sort of event this is supposed to lead up to?

Understanding this concept is important because of how we see globalism forced onto Western societies without their consent and also because it ties in with how literature or other tactics are used to revise the meaning of their identity or strip an entire nation of their sense of identity and erase them.

Let's Look at This From the Angle of Social Engineering

Do you think it's possible to erase an entire culture along with its people by repeatedly telling them they do not exist and denying recognition of their identity in all written and verbal statements? Well, it takes a long time and the people coordinating this type of agenda would make it a multigenerational project, but of course you can. In America, and in other Western societies, we see this very revision tactic woven into the literature that's being used in our education systems currently.

Pick any existing nation on the planet and just think about it. If you wanted to dissolve their nation, their cultural identity and completely erase them as a group, making sure their identity is no longer reinforced socially is a necessary step. But, you'll need to rename them and find something else to call them, as well as convince other people to go along with it. As stated previously in the chapter on color, the literature that's installed by the curriculum committee is worded in a way that does exactly that. It trains the students to refer to their host population by their color instead of referring to them by their national, ethnic or cultural identity. This begins the process of separating the host population from its own identity and dissolving it.

Now think about this. Every year, more and more students are trained to think and talk this way. This revision of the host populations identity is used more and more often in the academic material, media and social media until it eventually becomes normalized.

Use your own country as an example. Think about what happens when large numbers of other populations are imported to your society. And the generation coming in behind yours has been trained to think and talk in a way that negates the existence of your population. A small revision started by the literature used in schools is eventually transferred to all aspects of society, as the students graduate and take jobs in media, academia, political arena, legal system and so on. Eventually, your population will find itself saturated in material that uses its identity in a way that separates your population from it and delegitimizes your existence as a group.

So, what do you think happens once the number of people who use your populations identity in a way that reinforces it, is outnumbered by people who were trained to use it in a way that revises it and takes it away? Well, the other populations will support making the revision permanent as a way of validating themselves. They'll update the definition in the dictionary and the legal definition will eventually be changed. Now, your population no longer exists in the eyes of your own legal system. All of the books and media have been subtly reworded along the way and offer no evidence that your population is valid or ever existed. Members of your population can resort to arguing that they are valid and that they exist, but it's just their word against the generation coming in behind them, composed of those other populations who were imported. Together, they'll eventually outnumber your population. So, once the revision becomes legally binding and complete, there is no longer a unique identifier for your population. There is no unique name for your kind. Your population has been dispossessed of its own identity and no longer exists.

This concept is called *denial of identity* and it is used to debase our identity by routinely delegitimizing us socially in order to negate and invalidate our existence as a people.

Consider this. Would it seem strange to you if I were to distribute school literature in Africa, which was structured to call everything African, except for Black people? Does it seem equally strange that someone has structured the school literature in America, to call everything American except for White people?

Who Would Support Such an Agenda?

Rich globalists would support this type of agenda because it results in all of the different nations and identities being dissolved into one, homogenized global system and population that they can more easily control. Since it's done through language manipulation and revision, all of this can be achieved without taking time to change the laws and fight physical wars.

For those who are marxist, communist or antiwhite and want all White populations to be biologically erased. Their goal is to take that unique identity away from each population. They want to take the actual word that your population originated to encompass everything that makes you, and deny it to you. By denying recognition of it, they deny recognition of you as a people and negate your very existence. As time goes on, this leads to social displacement and will eventually result in dispossession and total erasure. This is one of the reasons they fight for control of the narrative. They want to ensure the literature has been worded to train others to stop reinforcing your identity and refer to your population using something else.

This type of revision is highly effective because most people assume the meaning of an identity based on the way they see it used publicly, and therefore accept that meaning. As this compounds with more and more people participating each year, it will eventually succeed at changing the actual speech pattern used by society. The revision gets pushed through various channels and normalized. This revision is introduced through ways, which are unannounced and very subtle. You'll see it built-in to the general remarks on public forums, scripted events and even in the random common literature that's broadcast and circulated in media or academia. It does not matter which social channel this revision comes through. And it does not matter where it is started, as the purpose is for it to spread, to saturate a society, to normalize it and eventually change what the general population thinks the identity means and the way they use it when they speak, think and write.

Let's use another country as an example. Consider Nigeria. Let's say that someone inside of their education system, either selects outside material that's already been worded this way, or rewords the material that's made there, so each year, little-by-little the students will be exposed to a larger volume of material that's worded to use the term Nigerian when referring to all other populations except for Black people. They'll be referred to by their color, as Black.

Combine this with the multiculturalism and diversity programs that we see forced on Western societies currently, and import populations and migrants from all around the world. Now, the original Nigerian host population has a generation coming in behind them composed of non-Black populations from all over the world. These immigrant populations, who have been trained in the schools there, now refer to every other population using the term Nigerian, except for Black people. This will spread as each year, more and more students are trained to think and talk in a way that separates the Nigerian host population from its own Nigerian identity, by referring to them as Black instead. This revision of the host population's identity will begin compounding as it's used more and more often in the academic material. And eventually it will be used in social media posts, as well as the mainstream media that is broadcast at the general population of Nigeria.

After enough time has passed, the original host population of Nigeria, who continue to use their Nigerian identity in a way that reinforces it, will become outnumbered by this multicultural generation coming in behind it, and who have been trained to use the Nigerian identity in a way that revises it and takes it away. Eventually, that multicultural generation coming in behind them grows up and begins to occupy all aspects of their society by holding jobs in Nigerian media, academia, political arena, the legal system and so on. Without even fully understanding the agenda they're participating in, that multicultural generation is now saturating the original Nigerian host population's country and culture from every angle. They structure verbal remarks, literature and media to use the Nigerian identity in a way that separates the Nigerian host population from it and delegitimizes the original Nigerian host population's existence as a group.

So, what do you think happens once the number of people, who use the host population's identity in a way that reinforces it, are outnumbered by people who were trained to use it in a way that revises it and takes it away from them? Simple. The Nigerian host population is taken over from the inside and eventually erased. Since this will benefit the multicultural populations, they will support permanently revising the definition of Nigerian as a way of validating themselves. They'll start renaming buildings and streets, tearing down statues or changing historical illustrations and adding people, who look like them into pictures or murals to give the impression that they have always been present in Nigeria. They'll update the definition of Nigerian in the dictionary and the legal definition will also get changed and then, that original Nigerian host population no longer exists in the eyes of their own legal system because the actual word that they used for their identity has been officially changed and taken away from them.

They'll find themselves in a situation where all of the books and media have been reworded and offer no evidence that they exist. They can resort to arguing if they want, but it's just their word against the multicultural generation coming in behind them, who have been trained to use the term Nigerian when referring to themselves and all other populations, except for Black people. So, the revision eventually becomes legally binding and complete. There is no longer a unique identifier for the original Nigerian host population. There is no ethnic, cultural or heritage-based name for them, they are no longer recognized in their own Nigerian legal system. They have been dispossessed of their own identity and their population will be permanently erased as they are greatly outnumbered and they disappear into a sea of global multicultural traffic.

That said, we don't currently see material used in schools that's been worded to call everything Nigerian or African except for Black people, but we do see material used in American schools that's worded to call everything American except for White people. We also see this material being used in other Western societies as the Irish are no longer being referred to as Irish, they're being referred to by their color instead, while all of the other recently installed populations are being referred to as Irish. The same with the French, Swedish,

Germans, English and so on. What started as a tiny or insignificant revision woven into the literature used in one small class like a special studies program, or defended in the name of "being inclusive" doesn't seem so tiny and insignificant anymore, does it?

Pay attention to how common this has become in universities, media and other social platforms where we're routinely told our population has no unique cultural identifier. We are told we must be a melting pot, and that our cultural identity does not exist and is just a social construct.

While attending classes, I noticed that all of the literature used at my school had been reworded so it no longer referred to me, my population or my heritage as American. And in cases where the literature did use the American identity, it used this identity in the most inside out and distorted way possible. Analyzing this pattern in all of the literature, the precision it's delivered with and the amount of internal coordination an agenda like this would require, the natural conclusion is that denial of identity was intentionally built-in to the material used at my school.

When a school exposes students to these lesson plans without telling them, *it results in a form of indirect teaching*. As an example, let's say a student is taking a biology class. The teacher uses literature that has this woven into it. While that student is focused on the main subject which is Biology, and is primarily focused on learning the terms or studying for the tests, without noticing it, they're also indirectly being trained to refer to their host population by their color, instead of referring to it as American. The student may not even notice this is taking place as their main focus is learning biology. As discussed in the previous chapter on color, through repetition and over a long enough period of time, the teacher trains the students to refer to their American host population by their color, instead of referring to it as American. This separates the American host population from its own American identity and begins the process of delegitimizing it and erasing it.

Watch for this pattern. Analyze your literature. Keep track of who's being referred to as American and who's not. Pay attention to the wording used on radio, television or in movies. Who are they referring to as the Americans, and who are they referring to by their color instead?

Consider the timing and coordination needed to roll this out in multiple Western societies at the same time. The literature used in their schools along with everything produced by mainstream media has been reworded to no longer refer to the Irish as Irish, the Swedish as Swedish or the French as French. Media will refer to people from all over the world who are pouring into those countries using those national, cultural or heritage-based identities, but not the native populations who originated them, and rely on them as an identifier of their culture, heritage and existence. Media routinely uses some broad, alternate or ambiguous term when referring to the native populations, but they refuse to use these cultural identities in a way that will reinforce them, and acknowledge them as the identity of the populations that originated them.

They won't do it because they want to revise the way society sees it used. They want to change the speech pattern of that society and disassociate the host population from its own identity by engaging in denial of identity. Just think how this all fits together on a large scale. With repetition, academia working in coordination with media, will do this long enough to normalize it and it will result in the dispossession of all Western national, cultural and heritage-based identities along with the erasure of all of the populations who originated them.

It is for the sake of our next generation that these revisions must be challenged and reversed. As well, the people who coordinate and promote this must be publicly confronted.

Student Action

Students have a very special role to play when challenging denial of identity. Since this material and training is being delivered through the education system, students are the only demographic who can internally challenge and purge this from inside of the schools. Students are in the belly of the beast. Students have a level of access that no one else has. The use of any literature containing this element can be disputed at the student level. Literature that uses a national, cultural or heritage-based identity in an inside out way, or denies its rightful recognition to the population who originated it, must be unanimously rejected. Students must no longer participate in normalizing or legitimizing these types of revisions in any way.

If your teacher is using literature where this element is present, bring this to their attention. Reiterate that the American identity was originated by our population and intended to be used as a unique identifier of our culture, heritage and our population. Explain that you don't want to be immersed in literature that uses our identity in an inside out way or in a way that separates our population from it.

Separately, let's begin the process of institutional change. To get your school to change the literature they use, students must file a request directly with the Dean of curriculum and curriculum committee. Since they are the ones who select the pool of literature that teachers can choose from, this message needs to be delivered to them directly. Discuss some of the talking points from this chapter. Check to ensure they understand why you will no longer participate, validate or be pressured to help them normalize the use of your identity in an inside out way or in a way that will disassociate you and your population from it. On these grounds, you can enter a demand with the school administration to provide you with classes and literature structured to reinforce your identity, as the current material is not adequate.

That said, it's also important to challenge denial of identity outside of the education system as well. *The best way to challenge denial of identity is through assertion of identity.* Show others when you notice denial of identity being used by the media or embedded in random literature. Any one of us can take the time to correct someone's remarks if they use our identity in an inaccurate or inside out way. Let them know you noticed what they said. Also, take a few minutes to write a letter directly to the publisher or the media outlet of books or magazines requesting that they use your identity in a way that reinforces it, instead of in a way that revises it, in their future works.

Redefining Terms

Revising or creating alternative definitions for well-known words, terms and concepts is one purpose you will see radicalized academics use the education platform for. They take a well-known word or term that the general population understands to be bad, and make an alternative definition that allows them to apply that term to people who are not bad, and who operate under a different understanding of what that term means. These radicalized teachers train students to use the alternative definition, as a form of targeted agitation or as a shock tactic directed at the host population.

As an example, let's take the word rapist. Rapist is a well-known word with a lot of attached stigma that the general population knows to be bad and associates with bad acts. We can agree that nobody in the general population wants to be called a rapist. Now, let's say that I am a radical academic and I make an alternative definition for the lesson plans used at my school location to teach students that the definition of a rapist is "someone who hates White people." As I teach class after class, I can train more and more students to refer to anyone who shows a hatred or criticism of White people, as a rapist.

Just imagine the effect it has on the general population as these students go out into society and call people "rapists," at random. Anyone being called a rapist will think they're being accused of what the general population understands a rapist to mean, but the person making the accusation is not clarifying any of that for them. They're just using the word rapist the way they were trained to use it by the radical academics who constructed their school lesson plans.

The person being called a rapist will, of course, be harmed in all the ways that being accused of rape would harm someone. The use of this deceptive tactic has the ability to slander, cause financial or physical harm, get people fired and make them unemployable or worse. While the person doing all of the name calling can evade responsibility based on the technicality that they're using the alternative definition made up in academia, instead of the definition the general population knows and operates by. When the person being called a rapist argues that they are not a rapist, the students will argue that they are, in fact, a rapist. These arguments can go back and forth, over a long period of time without the subject ever coming up, that each of the people involved is using a different definition for the word rapist.

Radical academics use students for this purpose, as a means to their end, knowing it's a creative way to engineer confusion, conflict, destabilization and they view it as a form of activism. For this type of *linguistic manipulation* to be effective on the general population, the academics need to create a misunderstanding between the definition the students are trained to use and the definition the person being called this name thinks it means. Otherwise, most people would not waste time participating in such arguments or do things they normally wouldn't do, like make personal concessions or support harmful policies and laws in an attempt to clear themselves from such accusations. Some of the more common mainstream terms we see used in academia and mainstream media are listed below. Let's analyze what the general population thinks it's being accused of versus the alternative definition that students are trained to use by radical academics.

Supremacy

What people think they're being accused of: Claiming racial superiority above other races.

What they're actually being accused of: Being the largest or dominant population in a society. Also known as the host population or the founding population of a society.

For radical academics, who consider it a form of activism to cause confusion or manipulate language to engineer conflict, this is a popular term because they know that the general population thinks being accused of "supremacy" is being accused of claiming racial superiority and not the academic version of being a dominant population within their own society.

This is why you see articles saying things such as, "Teaching your kids to read upholds White supremacy." Or that the instinctual resistance to laws and policies structured to harm the White host population is referred to as upholding White supremacy, because it interferes with destabilizing, overthrowing and systemically destroying the existing White society. Even people who are not White are called White supremacists because they are interfering with the destabilization and destruction of the White host population and its society.

When radical academics train students to say certain things are the fault of White supremacy, it's just an alternative way of saying certain things are a problem because it's a White population that's hosting them. It's a coded way of publicly calling on various special treatment groups and other installed populations to unite against the White host population and work to overthrow it, from within its own society and institutions. How else can you convince migrants to unite and work to overthrow the White population that hosts them as an act of charity? Easy. Just use coded language and say you're fighting White supremacy.

Radicals could very easily word their remarks to say they feel something is the fault of the largest or dominant population that hosts them. But wording it that way would not carry the social stigma or cause the negative social effects they're looking for. So, they create alternative definitions for preexisting terms like supremacy to refer to anyone, who resists the destabilization and destruction of the White host population, knowing it carries the social stigma of promoting a racial superiority belief system, and will socially harm that person in all the ways that actually promoting a racial superiority belief system would.

It's also alarming to see politicians make blanket statements condemning White supremacy or attempt to outlaw White supremacy because they're not revealing which definition of supremacy they're using. The general population can be made to believe they're outlawing racial superiority belief systems which I'm sure they're fine with. However, if they use the alternative definition, they're actually making it illegal for the White host population to resist being overthrown and dissolved into globalism without consent. It's a Treasonous way to outlaw any resistance to globalism.

But aside from causing confusion and infighting among the general population, there are other reasons for revising the meanings of certain terms, like making existing laws function differently. Take the commonly used term racist. To gain support for publicly condemning racists or outlawing racism, the general population was immersed in media using the term racist or racism in a way that implied it means treating others poorly based on color or race. The media and examples shown to the general population, put most people under the impression that outlawing racism would set the same behavioral requirements for all populations and reduce conflict. So, they voted in favor of laws banning racism. After the laws were in place, and some time had passed, radicals used the academic platform to construct an alternative definition to the term racism. One that teaches it's impossible to be racist to White people.

Using the alternative definition created in academia, makes these laws function differently, so they no longer offer equal protection to the White host population. Instead, the accusation of racist is used to carry out one-sided attacks against the White host population, make extortion demands and use legal warfare tactics. The alternative definition also shields the attackers and other populations who will be installed in the future, by training them to argue it's impossible for them to be racist to White people.

Radicals figured out that they don't have to change the laws, they just have to change the definition of certain legal terms to change the way the laws function. By revising the definition of racist, from one that offers equal protection to all populations to an alternative definition, they're able to deny equal protection to the White host population. They can then discriminate against the White host population on the basis of race and argue that it's not racist for them to do so.

This is what radicals mean when they say their revolution will be complete once the language is made perfect. If the meaning of each term, which the host population relies on to defend itself within the legal system, is revised so none of the terms offer equal protection to the host population, then the language has been made perfect because it's now impossible for the host population to defend itself. This creates the system that allows the radicals to incrementally destroy the host population in a way that's not technically categorized as illegal. Think of it like a *language lock*. All of the words you use to defend yourself or to seek justice in the justice system have been redefined. The result? There is no word for what you need. Therefore, it's been made impossible to defend yourself or obtain justice.

That said, when dealing in legal matters there is a difference between referring to something as racially motivated versus saying something is "racist". Since academics revised the definition of racist to one stating it's impossible to be racist to White people, then don't use the term racist to describe racially motivated discrimination or acts of violence against White citizens. Word your remarks to say it was racially-motivated or call it antiwhite, but don't use the word racist as it will sabotage your case.

Whiteness

What people think it means: Based on the way it sounds, whiteness is assumed to be a reference to the White population. Thus, it's expected that anyone who hears the word White in this modified way will interpret it to mean something along the lines of White existence, which is supported by the way we see it used publicly.

What the people who use it mean: The alternative definitions made up in academia are constantly being revised, but I have encountered definitions that define whiteness as: "White people preserving or retaining power and control over their own society and institutions." Resisting subversion, destabilization, or the destruction of White people is referred to as upholding whiteness.

The term "whiteness" functions as a weaponized term because it allows the speaker to evade responsibility for their remarks. Based on the way it sounds, we know that when radicals say things like "abolish whiteness," the general population will interpret that to mean something different than the alternative definition the person making the statement will argue it means.

Think of the concept of speaking with a forked-tongue or double-speak.

The general population will interpret that as a call *to harm the White population* because that's what it sounds like it would mean. The person making that statement will evade accountability by arguing they use an alternative definition for whiteness, which they made up.

One thing to point out is that they can easily word their message in a way that wouldn't be conflated with a call to harm the White population, but clearly choose not to do so. They want the general population to interpret their message as a call to harm the White population, while simultaneously avoiding accountability by arguing they use a different definition than everyone else. It's a calculated form of attack.

White Nationalist

What people think it means: Being accused of advocating for a separate, all-White nation-state.

What the people who use it mean: Anyone who happens to be White and also wants to live in a nation-state structure, instead of living under a one-world, single, globalist system.

In reality, anyone can be a nationalist. Black people can be a nationalist. Brown people can be nationalists. Yellow people can be nationalist. This is because by definition a nationalist is someone who wants to live and operate in a nation-state structure. So, someone who happens to be White and also wants to live in a nation-state structure, can be called a White nationalist. You will see this broadcast from public platforms knowing that the general population will assume that the person it's referring to is advocating for a separate all-White nation, instead of just resisting the destruction of their nation and being dissolved into globalism. Same term, two different interpretations.

Who Would Support Using These Tactics?

Radicals and rich globalist use these tactics for their goals as they want to make an entire population malleable and unstable. The strategy of using these tactics is to avoid liability when making public calls to harm or slander people. Use a word or term that the general population will interpret to have a different meaning based on the way it sounds, than the meaning the person using it claims it has. It's making people look bad, by calling them terms the general population assumes are bad based on the way they sound, but then arguing the person making the statement uses an alternative meaning to the slanderous term being used. Then the argument continues, they should not be held accountable for their audience interpreting the statement to mean something different.

We see installed populations trained to call members of the host population terms that nobody would want to be called. On a massive scale, these tactics are used to execute large-scale redistributions and pressure the host population to surrender everything that is theirs. Jobs, scholarships, institutional access and more are all surrendered to an unrelated population that they never even agreed to host. Now you can see why rich globalists who want to dissolve all borders, all nations and eventually all identities, would support these radicals and the use of these methods to loot from a host population and redistribute it to the rest of the world. This is how they can install unrelated populations, then use them as a tool to dissolve an entire nation and bring about globalism without obtaining consent or fighting a physical war.

We've already seen publicly circulated videos of agents in other countries training groups of incoming migrants to call Americans "racist" as they charge across the border and invade. It's a preplanned shock tactic. We've also seen CEOs of big companies say they stand against "White supremacy" and practically wink at the audience while saying this. Consider this before you go buy your next smartphone or computer. Which definition of supremacy do you think these globalist CEOs are using? The one that condemns a racial superiority belief system? Or the alternative definition that is a coded call for the overthrow of the White host population and to dissolve their nation-state into a globalist system? I bet if someone were to ask one of these CEOs which definition they're using, they would refuse to answer.

Additional Terms to Consider

Think about the implied meaning or the way you have seen these used publicly.

Diverse or Diversity

Most people assume diverse means something is mixed or offers more than one variety, based on the way it sounds. But when the term diverse or diversity is used in policies or laws, it implies that diversity means everything except for the host population. As an example, other populations can form groups that are called diverse, even if they're homogenous and not mixed with other populations. Therefore, the organization is called "diverse" because it's different than, or not of, the host population. Installing a diversity policy in all schools and institutions is one way to block the host population from accessing its own institutions and globalize that society without seeking their consent. A diversity policy is just a divestment policy by another name. There's no difference in the way that they function. That said, based on the way it has been used, I stopped using the term diversity because it excludes me, and *started using the term "variety"* because that term includes me. In my opinion, telling members of any host population to say they "value diversity" is just an alternative way of getting people *to say they value everything except for themselves*, which seems like a messed-up trick to play on people.

Systemic Racism

Based on the way I see it used, the term "systemic racism" is used by unrelated populations who want to be quickly installed into the control positions of a host society. It's used to put pressure on host populations to forfeit the control positions of their own institutions to unrelated populations, who are taught to unite against the host population, and consider it a form of justice to cause harm to the host population. This supports a rapid infiltration and take-over strategy. This works in conjunction with plans to globalize a society and dissolve it without obtaining consent or fighting physical wars.

Minority

Based on the way it sounds, the general population thinks that the term minority is a reference to a small-sized population. When the general public hears the term minority used in laws and policies, they assume that those policies are structured to help out small-sized populations, and one day, will help their population if ever they become small in size. But in reality, that term is used to exclude the host population on a biological basis, and set up a plural legal system, as well as take resources and opportunities away from the host population and redistribute them to unrelated populations. Whomever decided the legal definition of the term "minority," did not structure it so it would update and change as the composition of the general population changes over time. The host population will never be considered a minority in their own legal system or receive protections under laws structured to protect minorities, no matter how small their population becomes in the future. Unless the federal definition of minority is manually updated. But why would installed populations support changing it to offer equal protection?

Racist

It seems like there are thousands of definitions being circulated and new ones being made up on a daily basis, but the most radical interpretation I have encountered came from a communist. Some communists believe that all of the different races should be destroyed by mixing them together into one, global homogenous population, as a way of dissolving all nations and bringing about a one-world communist system. They use the term racist to refer to anyone who resists any of the tactics used to dissolve their race. If you resist and won't let them deconstruct or dissolve your race, they call you a race(ist) because your resisting destruction and reinforcing the existence of your kind. This is why you see radicals refer to babies as racist, because the mere act of having babies replenishes your race and delays the destruction of it. This is why White-Ethnics are denied the same dedicated dating services and apps that other populations have. White-Ethnics are genetically recessive compared to other populations and radicals want them to be mixed away, not to make more White-Ethnic babies. Therefore, they accuse you of unconscious racism or perpetuating racism in hopes that you will stop creating more of your own kind, and die out.

As you continue to examine the use of these terms, you'll notice a common theme among them. First, what they all have in common is that they each take a preexisting term that the general population understands to have a different meaning, and make up an alternative definition which allows them to refer to average citizens using these derogatory terms. Secondly, each of these terms is used to cause harm or trouble for anyone who resists having their society destroyed from within and dissolved into globalism. Not only is this tactic used to confuse and harm the general population, but it's also used to get terms with questionable definitions coded into law, which can be redefined at a later date to change the way that law functions. It can then be used for legal warfare against the host population.

What you can do at the individual level is to stop participating in any discussion that uses terms like these while refusing to define them or ignoring existing definitions. The people leading discussions like these are just using you to validate their alternative definitions and help speak their revised definition into existence.

If somebody calls you one of these terms, respond by asking which definition they're using. When they refuse to reveal it, then tell them you are unable to respond to them until you know what it is they're accusing you of.

This causes a malfunction because they want you to operate by what you think that term means based on the way it sounds, and not the alternative definition they use. If they reveal the alternative definition they're using instead of allowing you to react based on the way the term sounds, they won't get the reaction or public conflict they're looking for. They rely on this misunderstanding in order for this tactic to work.

For political action, reach out to your local representatives and lawmakers to establish a legal course of action. Ask them, "Since schools are teaching that the term racist or racism is not the correct term to use for race-based discrimination or racially motivated attacks against White citizens, then what term are they suggesting we use for that concept?" Or, if they say that it is the correct term to use, remind them that the schools have been teaching that it's impossible to be racist to White people, so students are being trained to interpret existing laws or policies on racism in a way that does not offer equal protection to White citizens. That said, pressure your local representative and lawmakers to propose legislation and work on coding it into law to make it illegal to interpret terms like racist in a way that does not offer equal protection to White citizens. If they truly want to fix the justice system or make multiculturalism work, they should support such a request, right? The position they take should determine if they get your support or not.

Demand Equal Training

It's simple when you think about it. If the public attacks on our population will not be stopped, then we need dedicated equal training in order to defend ourselves and our population. If public platforms will be used to attack us as individuals and as a group, then we must be trained to defend ourselves as individuals and as a group.

We can see that radicals use multiculturalism for the purpose of creating agitation, destabilization and conflict. We can see that the reason they word their remarks or material using the tactics discussed in previous chapters, is because of the effect they want it to have on the general population.

They know that using public platforms to broadcast prosecutorial statements, cropped narratives and smearing people using derogatory terms that they refuse to define is a creative way to get backlash and revenge attacks carried out against White citizens. We see large media companies engage in one-sided reporting. In addition, they crop news stories by redacting details and begin or end the stories at the spot that's needed to construct an alternative narrative, which will incite backlash or revenge attacks against White citizens. Meanwhile, the people orchestrating it get to remain anonymous and continue to cause trouble. Over and over again, they have shown us that they will use these tactics for personal enjoyment and to make things more unstable and worse for the whole population year after year. And they will call it "progress" while they do it.

You may ask: Can we simply disassociate from the other populations we see this marketed to and avoid conflict that way? The answer is no. Relocating to a different area is ridiculed as "White flight." Before these tactics were introduced in the school system, laws were passed to block White-Ethnics from having their own communities or institutions by categorizing them as non-diverse. Then, diversity quota requirements were put in place to install other populations, who get trained to use these tactics on White citizens. Taxpayer money and government programs are provided under the banner of affordable housing or other misleading titles to target and occupy poor or working-class White-Ethnic communities with the other populations. Besides forced-association, this nullifies the White populations vote because it's usually paired with identity politics. It also makes it impossible for White-Ethnics to keep a safe distance and to reconstitute their own secure and stable communities. Not only are we forced to host other populations in our institutions and communities, we are constantly shown that laws on hate crimes, racial motive crimes or terrorism will not be applied to those who attack White citizens. And mainstream media has been instructed not to report on them.

That said, most of us realize that populations left to function on their own essentially make an effort to get along peacefully. You'll see people use good manners or attempt to be helpful when interacting with others in public. But what makes our situation different is that we have people who are openly dedicated to using large public platforms to instigate perpetual conflict. Individual acts of kindness are so minor in comparison that they're no match for undoing the negative social effects caused by the narratives these large platforms broadcast on a daily basis.

Can the school make certain teachers stop using this type of material? It's impossible. Academic freedom shields teachers who select literature containing these properties. For the record, I do not advocate taking away the rights and freedoms of others. I think the best way to neutralize the effect these tactics have is to make them publicly visible. Establishing equal training at each school location where this material is used, or one of these teachers is present, can disable their manipulation and instigation tactics without taking away anybody's rights and freedoms.

Students enter this demand directly with the school administration. They don't have to speak about this publicly or gain the support of the student body. In the event, the school administration does not honor the rights and freedoms of White students or engages in acts of obstruction or intimidation. Students must seek off-campus legal help to confront that behavior.

What Should Equal Training Mean?

When thinking about what equal training means, we need to take into consideration the concepts discussed in the previous chapters. They have been used over a long period of time to condition the general population. Thus, we need to understand our starting point.

We're starting at a point where the use of cropped narratives and literature that's been worded to group a population together by racial category or color category and put it on trial has been one-sided, and this has installed a one-sided worldview in the mind of the general population. This worldview needs to get balanced out. We need to acknowledge that what the other populations have been trained to call our population is different from what our population has been trained to call theirs. The way the other populations have been trained to talk to, and about, our population is different from the way our population has been trained to talk to, and about, theirs.

Currently, if we find ourselves in a class where the material used is structured to put our racial or color category "on trial," we have not been trained to construct our counterarguments and deliver our defense. So, we automatically get framed for whatever crimes they're charging our population with. The same thing happens in politics, where we get targeted with rhetoric that's structured to put our racial or color category on trial and make extortion demands based on aggressive accusations. We have not been trained to construct our counterarguments and deliver our defense, so we automatically lose in the eyes of the public.

These displays are then used to support the approval of policies and laws that harm our population or steal from it and transfer it to the accusers. We see the same situation when evaluating media. Whether it's a hit piece presented as an opinion article, a fictional story, or a large-scale movie production that is structured to frame our entire racial or color category, we have no training to formulate an effective response and deliver a defense. So, we automatically appear guilty in the eyes of the general population. This, in turn, is then used to publicly support policies and laws structured to harm our population and steal from it or encourage revenge attacks against random White citizens using coded language and terms like "racial justice."

Consider the long-term, one-sided use of these tactics in academia along with large media platforms. Just imagine what's been installed into the mind of the general population and how it's been conditioned over time.

Academic Focus

Within academia and the broader education system, equal training means establishing a space that is dedicated to teaching White students about the most common tactics they will see directed at their population from public platforms. Students need to have interactive discussions about encounters with others who use these tactics and share best practices for avoiding conflict and de-escalating certain situations.

Equal training is about disclosing the tactics used at their specific school location, the teachers who use them, and the subjects they've been embedded into. It's about using current samples of the material used at that location, as a teaching instrument, by studying the structures within it, along with the behavioral effects it has on the groups it's marketed to. It's about training White students to neutralize the negative social impacts caused by material present at their location. It's about studying the structure of antiwhite policies and laws, as well as antiwhite thought and belief systems.

Equal training is about offering the same level of complete immersion learning. Teach White students to complete oral or written assignments using the same methods and language structures that maneuver collective responsibility based on color category, racial category, or another relevant group-based identity. Provide the same level of access, hands-on training and public support when presenting these writings or assignments on public platforms, such as the student newspaper, and ensuring they're given the same opportunity to circulate their work through shared academic networks globally. Start the long process of equalizing the existing academic cache by ensuring the application of subjects discussed in previous chapters no longer remain one-sided.

Equal training is about ensuring that students, who find themselves in a situation where a teacher is putting them (or their group) on trial or has selected material that's been structured to put them (or their group) on trial, have the experience they need to formulate their counterarguments and deliver an effective defense on behalf of themselves and their group. Equal training is about training students how to reject teachers who pressure them to validate revisions, cropped narratives or other concepts they disagree with.

It's about training students to operate from a position of strength when opting out of assignments or dialogue that revises the name of their rights to privileges or pressures them to use terms like "racism," "supremacy" and "oppression" while refusing to define them. Train students how to reject and block teachers from using their position of authority or any form of retaliation to make students validate their revisions and cropped narratives or assist them in speaking their concepts into existence.

Equal training also means training White students how to map out the networks present at their location. Research the authors of material containing these properties along with the people who coordinated the instillation and use of this material at their location. Take an inventory of the people and organizations involved. As well, research their background and analyze for their motive.

Consider the additional criteria listed below. What would you add or remove based on the needs in your area?

- Train White students how to adequately document and evidence situations that must be pursued through the legal system.
- Train White students how to have laws enforced at school locations that only enforce laws on behalf of minorities and do not enforce the law on behalf of White students.

- Train White students to reinforce and defend their sense of identity and existence at school locations where they're told White people should not or do not exist.
- Train White students to exercise their rights and freedoms like protesting, forming on-campus student organizations, and peaceful assembly.

White students need to work together and create a clear pathway at each school by identifying teachers who use these tactics, so other students have the ability to obtain all required classes without being made to interact with these teachers or the students they market these tactics to. It's important that students can focus on their actual core subjects like Math, Biology, etc., and not be continuously disadvantaged by creative forms of harassment and targeted agitation. This will create a pathway for White students to liberate themselves through equal training.

Media Focus

When focusing on the media, remember that we're in a narrative-driven environment where different groups can be activated by using the tactics discussed in previous chapters. Focus on the tactics used by certain media companies to manipulate the combined media cache and redact the record that's left for our next generation. For example, as you catch specific media platforms diminishing the crimes against White citizens by excluding them from mainstream reporting, then you'll want to look for ways to offset the imbalance that creates. Use alternative platforms to ensure these events are fully documented and publicly reported. Ensure the descriptions of those involved are not redacted out and an accurate record is made for our existing population, as well as our next generation.

Don't let the media create a one-sided record that will be used to sabotage our next generation by using one-sided reporting, redaction, and censorship tactics.

We've already been shown that the collective media cache will be used to support arguments that group our population together on the basis of racial category or color category and put it on trial. Our next generation will need a documented media cache of equal size and detail to draw on when they construct their counterarguments and deliver their defense. They can't be left with a media cache that uses the term "White people" billions of times but uses "youths, teens, protestors, people in search of a different life, etc.," for everyone else.

This conceals the information they'll need to defend themselves in future negotiations that touch on race, color and group-based accountability, because one side will have documented evidence, but not the other. Those descriptions must be made a part of the permanent record to ensure the record left for our next generation is not one-sided and they are not sabotaged or set up to lose in future negotiations involving race, color, tribe and atonement.

Call out articles that redact certain details or the evidencing of crimes committed against White citizens and label them as deficient. Redacting color, racial or tribal identity of the attackers is a creative way of denying White citizens equal protection under laws pertaining to color or racially motivated crimes as well as inhibiting the ability to evaluate and determine the true motive. Think about it. How can you say an attack was motivated by race or color if race and color are redacted out from the documentation you present in a court and replaced with a vague descriptor like a "youth?"

The Importance of Self-Representation

You can't possibly expect to be fairly represented by other groups who have been trained to unite based on their shared resentment of the White population. We need self-representation to be restored in all aspects *and at every level* of our own institutions and society.

Consider how antiwhite literature is marketed to the other populations by pairing it with various special studies programs, then hiring quotas are used to install people from those groups into control positions in all aspects of our society and institutions. Equal protection under the law will usually be overridden by their tribal loyalty to one another. White citizens will inevitably find themselves in the courtroom of a Judge who was taught that "it's impossible to be racist to White people." Or at the mercy of a jury composed of various special-treatment groups, who were taught to unite with each other and work as a team to harm the White population. Or living in the region of a District Attorney who happens to be a member of the same special treatment group as the person who committed a crime. In this case, they will drop the criminal charges as an act of solidarity, and so on. In the legal system, you're going to find yourself in situations where you're using terms and definitions that offer equal protection to White citizens, but the Judge, DA or other legal representatives are using alternative definitions that deny equal protection to White citizens. Our population must be trained on how to properly navigate the legal system and obtain justice in this type of environment.

First and foremost, we need our own legal representation and dedicated legal network. It should no longer be the decision of those taught with antiwhite material and ideology to decide whether or not we receive equal protection under the law. Currently, there is no true evaluation of the motive for acts of violence or attacks that are carried out against our population. There is no law that requires the schools or police to automatically categorize attacks on our population as racially motivated or as a hate crime the way it does for minorities. Therefore, they don't. The evaluation for motive never happens and equal protection under the law does not occur. This is because equal protection under these laws won't be obtained without self-representation and conducting a true evaluation for motive as well as presenting the evidence in a court.

It's useless for us to report attacks to school officials or local police departments because they don't have a legal obligation to protect White citizens. Until it is explicitly coded into law and worded in a way that cannot be interpreted to deny equal protection to the White population, we must form our own networks to perform these functions.

As stated in the introduction, I was exploring legal options and noticed it was impossible to locate an attorney willing to represent me because most attorneys specialize in legal cases representing minorities. We need to work with our local representatives on legislation and laws to establish a dedicated legal network as well as establish somewhere to evidence and report any acts of obstruction. Anyone blocking us from establishing a dedicated legal network is doing so as a way to deny us access to our own justice system and equal protection under the law, which should not be permitted.

Political Action—Local Level

Think about each of the tactics discussed in previous chapters, along with the negative social effects they have on the general population. Think of all of the conflict each of these tactics cause. Now consider this. Any politician, who truly wanted to make diversity and multiculturalism work, and to see multiple different populations succeed at living peacefully alongside one another, would not structure their writings or public remarks using these tactics. When you encounter politicians who claim to "value diversity" while simultaneously using any of these tactics to create conflict, that gives you enough information to confirm that *they're lying to you.* They're speaking with a forked tongue.

Audit your local representatives and take an inventory of politicians who have used these tactics to cause destabilization. Document it by getting a copy of anything distributed in writing or a recording if they delivered it in public remarks or a speech. Build a file that can be shared locally and used to confront them when the time comes. Use this as evidence to get them voted out and replaced with someone who will genuinely represent the will of our population.

Up until now, they have been one-sided about supporting legislation or laws that mention race or color and are reluctant to do the same for our population. For social restabilization to occur, this must end. Explain to your representative that the reason current and future political action will involve race or color moving forward is because the education system along with the media apparatus made it about race and color when they worked together to unite all of the other populations against our population. We have been subjected to remarks about race or color when being told that specific laws do not protect us or being denied entry to our own institutions, jobs and opportunities. Radicalized politicians made it about race or color when introducing legislation structured to harm our population and when concerns were raised, they said that was "a good thing."

Tell them that if they're not comfortable representing the needs and the political will of White citizens then that's a sign they're in the wrong line of work and must find something else to do. White citizens don't want one of our political slots to be wasted on someone who refuses to publicly challenge antiwhite rhetoric, policies, and laws.

Think of criteria and demands that political representatives must meet in order to obtain your support. I have listed a few examples below, but edit this and tailor it to the needs of your area. Politicians who want White citizens to vote for them must:

1.   Support the establishment of a unique identifier for our populations. Require the official recognition of White-Ethnics.

2.   Support the establishment of equal training programs for White students at all schools located in their district.

3.   Support the hiring of White-Ethnic school staff and work to restore a classic, Western education curriculum offering for White students.

4.   Work to restore proportionate access to all schools, staff positions, government agencies, social services, scholarships, grants and other opportunities.

5.   Work to repeal and replace laws structured to deny equal protection to White citizens.

6.   Conduct an official review of laws and policies that were used to displace White citizens from their own institutions and leadership roles in society. Then work on repealing those laws and policies.

7.   Introduce policies and laws aimed at restoring self-representation at all levels of our society and all institutions that were founded by our population and intended for the betterment of our population.

8.   Work to repeal all existing laws and policies that categorize discrimination of White citizens as "positive discrimination."

9.   Work to absolve White citizens from laws that were structured to deny equal protection to them.

Separately, we need a close evaluation of the system that is designed to cause us harm. And we need to educate our population on existing laws, as most of us are living under a legal caste system and don't even realize it. Look closely and you will find that slowly but surely, there is a second legal framework that has been constructed using biologically based legal terms. Most people see the term "minority" used and based on the way it sounds or the way they commonly see it used among their peers, think it's a reference to the size of a population, meaning being minor in comparison to other populations. They believe that one day when their population becomes smaller compared to the other populations, they'll automatically be considered a minority in the legal system and offered all of the same protections as other groups. That is incorrect.

When dealing in the legal system or the passing of laws and legislation, the definition of minority that is used is a fixed biological term that excludes White-Ethnic populations, regardless of what percentage of the general population they make up currently or in the future. Let's use sample verbiage from a piece of California legislation as an example. Look at the way it is worded. Has it been worded to offer equal protection to all populations? No, it has not. Who does it offer protection to? It offers protection to minorities. Who is considered a minority? The federal definition of minority determines which populations are categorized as a minority. The populations not on the list are not considered a minority. Therefore, they are not offered equal protection under laws and legislation structured like this:

115TH CONGRESS
1ST SESSION
S. RES. 118

Condemning hate crime and any other form of racism, religious or ethnic bias, discrimination, incitement to violence, or animus targeting a minority in the United States.

Federal Guidelines for Definition as a Minority

***Definition is from Title VII of the Civil Rights Act of 1964, which uses Equal Employment Opportunity Form EEO-1.

A.) **Black (not of Hispanic origin)** – All persons having origins in any of the Black racial groups of Africa.

B.) **Hispanic** – All persons of Mexican, Puerto Rican, Cuban, Central or South American, or other Spanish culture of origin, regardless of race.

C.) **Asian or Pacific Islander** – All persons having origins in any of the original peoples of the Far East, Southeast Asia, the Indian subcontinent or the Pacific Islands. This area includes, for example, China, India, Japan, Korea, the Philippine Islands and Samoa.

D.) **American Indian or Alaskan Native** – All persons having origins in any of the original peoples of North America, and who maintain cultural identification through tribal affiliation or community recognition.

If you look closely, you will see that most laws and policies have been structured to offer one-sided protection to minorities. It's by making no mention of the White host population that they are able to deny equal protection to us. This explains the one-sided censorship you see in media and social media platforms. If the laws on the books say they are only obligated to offer protection to minorities, then they only censor criticism directed at minorities. They are not required to censor criticism directed at the White population or censor minorities when they criticize the White population because these laws were structured to leave the White population unprotected. So, while the general population is left scratching their heads, trying to figure out why verbal attacks directed at the White population are permitted, the high-level politicians and media executives remain silent and pretend not to know why, instead of explaining that it's precisely for this reason. This entire time, they have allowed attacks on the White population to continue. They're probably hoping that the general population does not figure it out before it's too late to get the laws repealed or changed so they offer equal protection. You'll see the same thing with the language used in so-called equity laws. It's by making no mention of the White population that nothing is left for it.

When looking closely, we can see that lawmakers and politicians can very easily structure laws to offer proportionate access or equal protection to all populations but many of them choose not to. That gives us enough information to confirm that this was done intentionally. Research who sponsored and endorsed resolutions and laws structured this way and ensure everyone around you learns what they did.

Put your local political representatives on the spot in a publicly visible way. Ask them, "Are the existing laws simply outdated, or is denying proportionate access and equal protection to White citizens something that's being coordinated on purpose?"

That said, if you encounter politicians or organizations who oppose equal protection for White citizens, it's because they want to keep using these tactics to harm the White population and steal from it. Politicians, who block the establishment of legal representation dedicated to our population, drafting new copies of existing laws to offer us equal protection, or absolving our population from laws that do not provide equal protection, are promoting the use of a legal caste system and engaging in legal warfare against their own citizenry. Currently, there is no legal obligation for schools, police, or state agencies to shield White citizens from attacks or enforce the law on behalf of White citizens, therefore they don't. Nothing changes *until the laws get changed* and equal protection for the White population is coded into law and strictly enforced.

Printed in the USA
CPSIA information can be obtained
at www.ICGtesting.com
CBHW062008300624
10903CB00021B/745